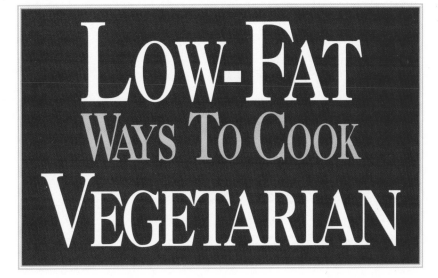

LOW-FAT
WAYS TO COOK
VEGETARIAN

LOW-FAT
WAYS TO COOK
VEGETARIAN

COMPILED AND EDITED BY
SUSAN M. MCINTOSH, M.S., R.D.

Oxmoor
House®

Library of Congress Catalog Number: 96-67710
ISBN: 0-8487-2206-X
Manufactured in the United States of America
First Printing 1996

Editor-in-Chief: Nancy Fitzpatrick Wyatt
Editorial Director, Special Interest Publications: Ann H. Harvey
Senior Foods Editor: Katherine M. Eakin
Senior Editor, Editorial Services: Olivia Kindig Wells
Art Director: James Boone

LOW-FAT WAYS TO COOK VEGETARIAN

Menu and Recipe Consultant: Susan McEwen McIntosh, M.S., R.D.
Assistant Editor: Kelly Hooper Troiano
Assistant Foods Editor: Caroline A. Grant, M.S., R.D.
Copy Editor: Shari K. Wimberly
Editorial Assistants: Julie A. Cole, Valorie J. Cooper
Indexer: Mary Ann Laurens
Assistant Art Director: Cynthia R. Cooper
Designer: Carol Damsky
Senior Photographer: Jim Bathie
Photographers: Howard L. Puckett, *Cooking Light* magazine;
  Ralph Anderson
Senior Photo Stylist: Kay E. Clarke
Photo Stylists: Cindy Manning Barr, *Cooking Light* magazine;
  Virginia R. Cravens
Production and Distribution Director: Phillip Lee
Associate Production Managers: Theresa L. Beste, Vanessa D. Cobbs
Production Coordinator: Marianne Jordan Wilson
Production Assistant: Valerie Heard

Our appreciation to the staff of *Cooking Light* magazine and to the Southern
Progress Corporation library staff for their contributions to this book.

Cover: *Layered Vegetable Lasagna (recipe on page 95)*
Frontispiece: *Black and White Beans with Orzo (recipe on page 100)*

CONTENTS

NEW VEGETARIAN BASICS

*W*hat's the prescription for healthy eating? Lots of whole grains, fruits, and vegetables, the basics of a vegetarian diet. Whether you have already adopted a vegetarian lifestyle or just want one or two veggie meals each week, read on. There's a recipe for every taste and plenty of health-smart ideas as well.

Meals without meat are catching on in America, and with good reason. People across the country are aware that those who eat more fruits, vegetables, legumes, and whole grain breads and cereals are less likely to develop cancer, heart disease, and other health problems.

You may not think of yourself as a vegetarian. But if you are cutting back on the portion sizes of meat or sometimes serving meals without meat, you are already benefiting from this healthy way of eating and could be considered an occasional vegetarian.

The majority of vegetarians fall in the group called **lacto-ovo vegetarians** because they do eat milk products (lacto) and eggs (ovo) in addition to vegetables, legumes, fruits, grains, seeds, and nuts. **Lacto vegetarians** consume milk and dairy products along with plant foods, while **ovo vegetarians** eat eggs along with their plant food diets.

In contrast, **vegans** eat only plant foods. They do not eat meat, milk products, eggs, poultry, fish, or other animal products.

Whatever your category, you'll enjoy *Low-Fat Ways To Cook Vegetarian*. No special cooking techniques are required, and you'll find the ingredients to be familiar ones. Best of all, these recipes are great-tasting—and they're good for you.

SCIENCE SAYS . . .

For years, health authorities have praised the benefits of a vegetarian diet. The American Dietetic Association reported in 1993 that many scientific studies have suggested a vegetarian diet may reduce the risk of several chronic diseases and conditions, including "obesity, coronary artery disease, hypertension, diabetes mellitus, and some types of cancer."

The 1995 edition of the U. S. Department of Agriculture's *Dietary Guidelines for Americans* states that vegetarian diets are consistent with USDA's guidelines for healthy eating. The USDA also reports that vegetarians can meet the Recommended Dietary Allowances for nutrients when they eat appropriate amounts of a variety of foods.

The health benefits of a vegetarian diet are based on the basic nature of fruits, vegetables, legumes, and grains—they are generally low in fat but high in fiber and essential vitamins and minerals.

Dark green leafy vegetables, dark yellow and orange vegetables, and citrus fruits are rich in the antioxidants beta carotene and vitamins C and E. Antioxidants are thought to help protect against some types of cancer and heart disease.

VEGETARIAN NUTRITION

If you are an occasional vegetarian, you may think that you need to add meat to your diet in order to get the proper amount of nutrients, especially protein. However, this concern is unfounded.

• **Protein.** Vegetables, grains (bread, cereal, pasta, and rice), nuts, and seeds all contain some protein. Legumes, such as dried beans, lentils, and split peas, are especially high in protein. To get a balanced diet with plenty of protein, eat a variety of legumes, grains, and vegetables. When eaten over the course of a day, the plant proteins complement each other to provide the high-quality protein required by the body.

Milk products and/or eggs are very high in protein, and even small amounts enhance the quality of vegetable protein. If you are a vegan and choose not to eat milk and eggs, include tofu (soy protein) regularly. It is comparable in protein value to meat.

Ensure a healthy diet by eating a variety of fruits, vegetables, and grains daily.

Soft tofu is perfect for use in dips and spreads. Firm tofu can be cut up and added to stir-fries, salads, and casseroles.

Follow the Daily Food Guide on page 8 to make sure you get necessary protein and other nutrients.

• **Iron.** Skeptics of a vegetarian lifestyle often question whether a vegetarian will receive enough iron from a nonmeat diet. It is true that the iron in meat (heme iron) is more readily absorbed than the iron in nonmeat sources such as vegetables and grains (nonheme iron). Still, studies show that vegetarians in the United States are at no greater risk of anemia than meat-eaters. Perhaps that's because vegetarians get plenty of vitamin C, which is found in several fruits and vegetables. Vitamin C (ascorbic acid) increases the absorption of nonheme iron.

The following foods are considered good vegetable sources of iron: whole grain and fortified cereals, legumes, dark green vegetables, nuts and seeds, and dried fruits such as prunes, dates, figs, and raisins.

• **Calcium.** Dairy products, such as cheese and yogurt, are excellent sources of calcium. If you are a vegan and don't eat dairy products, you must obtain this essential mineral from other sources. Calcium is found in some dark green vegetables, such as collard and turnip greens, and it is abundant in tofu that has been processed with calcium sulfate.

• **Zinc.** Meat and other animal products are major sources of zinc, a mineral necessary for proper growth and development. Zinc is also found in grains, nuts, and legumes as well as in wheat germ.

• **Vitamin B_{12}.** Because this vitamin is found only in foods of animal origin, there is valid concern about a vitamin B_{12} deficiency in vegans who eat no animal products of any kind. To be safe, vegans should eat foods fortified with vitamin B_{12} (some breakfast cereals, soy beverages, and some brands of nutritional yeast) or take a B_{12} supplement daily. Lacto and ovo vegetarians who consume milk, yogurt, and cheese should not have a problem with vitamin B_{12} deficiency.

• **Vitamin D.** This vitamin is also lacking in plant foods. But vitamin D is unique in that it can be made by the human body after exposure to sunlight. Vegetarians with little exposure to sunlight should consume vitamin D-fortified milk or soy milk or take a vitamin D supplement.

INFANTS AND CHILDREN

Rapidly growing infants, children, and adolescents need large amounts of calories for proper growth. Vegetarian diets are generally higher in bulk yet lower in fat and calories than nonvegetarian diets. Care should be taken that sufficient calories are provided to support growth. These age groups also need a source of vitamins D and B$_{12}$ and need to eat plenty of foods high in calcium, iron, and zinc.

Pregnant and lactating women can also receive adequate nutrients from a vegetarian diet but must plan to include a variety of protein-rich plant foods and sufficient calories to meet the high energy demands of pregnancy and breast-feeding. A physician may prescribe nutritional supplements.

MEAL PLANNING

To achieve a balanced, healthy vegetarian diet, the American Dietetic Association recommends the following:

• Limit the intake of low nutrient-dense foods such as sweets and fatty foods.

• Choose whole or unrefined grain products instead of refined, or use fortified or enriched cereal products.

• Eat a variety of fruits and vegetables, including a good food source of vitamin C.

• Use low-fat or nonfat milk and dairy products.

• Limit egg yolks to three to four per week.

• Have a reliable source of vitamin B$_{12}$ if you're a vegan. These include fortified commercial breakfast cereals, a fortified soy beverage, or a vitamin B$_{12}$ supplement each day. Vitamin D supplements may be necessary if exposure to sunlight is limited.

DAILY FOOD GUIDE FOR VEGETARIANS

Food Group	Suggested Daily Serving	Serving Sizes
Breads, cereals, rice, and pasta	6 or more	1 slice bread ½ bun or bagel ½ cup cooked cereal ½ cup cooked rice or pasta 1 ounce dry cereal
Vegetables	4 or more	½ cup cooked 1 cup raw
Legumes and other meat substitutes	2 to 3	½ cup cooked dry beans 4 ounces tofu or tempeh 1 cup soy milk 2 tablespoons nuts or seeds (use sparingly because these tend to be high in fat)
Fruits	3 or more	1 piece fresh fruit ¾ cup fruit juice ½ cup canned fruit ½ cup cooked fruit
Dairy products	Optional—up to 3 servings daily	1 cup skim milk 1 cup nonfat or low-fat yogurt 1½ ounces low-fat cheese
Eggs	Optional— limit to 3 to 4 yolks per week	1 egg or 2 egg whites
Fats, sweets, and alcohol	Limited	

Copyright The American Dietetic Association. Reprinted by permission from *Journal of the American Dietetic Association*, Volume 93, Number 11.

Fat Alert

Although most vegetarian foods are low in fat, saturated fat, and cholesterol, added ingredients can change those values. Margarine, oil, nuts, seeds, nut and seed butters, avocados, and olives are all high in fat. Whole milk dairy products and egg yolks are also high in fat, much of which is saturated. Limit such ingredients to keep calories from fat under 30 percent.

LOW-FAT BASICS

*W*hether you are trying to lose or maintain weight, low-fat eating makes good sense. Research studies show that decreasing your fat intake reduces risks of heart disease, diabetes, and some types of cancer. The goal recommended by major health groups is an intake of 30 percent or less of total daily calories.

The *Low-Fat Ways To Cook* series gives you practical, delicious recipes with realistic advice about low-fat cooking and eating. The recipes are lower in total fat than traditional recipes, and most provide less than 30 percent of calories from fat and less than 10 percent of calories from saturated fat.

If you have one high-fat item during a meal, you can balance it with low-fat choices for the rest of the day and still remain within the recommended percentage. For example, fat contributes 45 percent of the calories in Garden Greens Salad for the Colorful Company Brunch menu beginning on page 12. However, because the salad and dressing are served with other low-fat foods, the total menu provides only 20 percent of calories as fat.

The goal of fat reduction need not be to eliminate all fat from your diet. In fact, a small amount of fat is needed to transport fat-soluble vitamins and maintain other normal body functions.

FIGURING THE FAT

The easiest way to achieve a diet with 30 percent or fewer of total calories from fat is to establish a daily "fat budget" based on the total number of calories you need each day. To estimate your daily calorie requirements, multiply your current weight by 15. Remember that this is only a rough guide because calorie requirements vary according to age, body size, and level of activity. To gain or lose 1 pound a week, add or subtract 500 calories a day. (A diet of fewer than 1,200 calories a day is not recommended unless medically supervised.)

Once you determine your personal daily caloric requirement, it's easy to figure the number of fat grams you should consume each day. These should equal or be lower than the number of fat grams indicated on the Daily Fat Limits chart.

DAILY FAT LIMITS

Calories Per Day	30 Percent of Calories	Grams of Fat
1,200	360	40
1,500	450	50
1,800	540	60
2,000	600	67
2,200	660	73
2,500	750	83
2,800	840	93

NUTRITIONAL ANALYSIS

Each recipe in *Low-Fat Ways To Cook Vegetarian* has been kitchen-tested by a staff of qualified home economists. Registered dietitians have determined the nutrient information, using a computer system that analyzes every ingredient. These efforts ensure the success of each recipe and will help you fit these recipes into your own meal planning.

The nutrient grid that follows each recipe provides calories per serving and the percentage of calories from fat. In addition, the grid lists the grams of total fat, saturated fat, protein, and carbohydrate, and the milligrams of cholesterol and sodium per serving. The nutrient values are as accurate as possible and are based on these assumptions.

• When the recipe calls for cooked pasta, rice, or noodles, we base the analysis on cooking without additional salt or fat.

• Only the amount of marinade absorbed by the food is calculated.

• Garnishes and other optional ingredients are not calculated.

• Some of the alcohol calories evaporate during heating, and only those remaining are counted.

• When a range is given for an ingredient (3 to 3½ cups, for instance), we calculate the lesser amount.

• When the recipe calls for vegetable broth, we analyze for canned broth which contains salt.

• Fruits and vegetables listed in the ingredients are not peeled unless specified.

Gazpacho Pasta, Ginger-Berry Tossed Salad, and Tangy French Bread (menu on page 20)

SENSIBLE MEALS

*V*egetarian meals generally have the benefit of being high in vitamins, minerals, and fiber while being quite low in fat. The secret is in the choice of ingredients and methods of preparation.

The following menus can give you ideas on how to plan complete vegetarian meals. Just remember to include a variety of vegetables, grains, and fruit. By eating different foods, you will benefit from the protein and vitamin make-up of each. For instance, the soup in the Rustic Italian Supper menu (page 15) contains protein from both beans and pasta, while the biscuits and dessert round out the meal with additional protein and other nutrients.

Each menu in this chapter is based on a main dish that contributes at least 10 grams of protein per serving. Refer to the chart on page 8 for information on how many servings of various foods you need to eat every day to achieve a healthy level of nutrients.

COLORFUL COMPANY BRUNCH

Invite a few friends over for a casual morning brunch. Here's a meatless menu that's hearty enough to delight vegetarians and nonvegetarians alike.

Uncomplicated preparation enhances the garden-fresh flavors of tomatoes, zucchini, lettuce, and sweet red peppers. Most of these recipes may be prepared well in advance, leaving only the frittata to assemble and cook after guests arrive.

Cheddar Potato Frittata

Garden Greens Salad

Melon with Sweet Onion Dressing

Zucchini-Orange Bread

Coffee

Serves 6
TOTAL CALORIES PER SERVING: 362
(CALORIES FROM FAT: 20%)

CHEDDAR POTATO FRITTATA

By using egg substitute instead of regular eggs, you reduce the cholesterol from 213 milligrams to only 6 milligrams.

1½ cups (about ½ pound) coarsely chopped
    round red potato
Vegetable cooking spray
1 cup chopped tomato
¼ cup chopped green onions
½ teaspoon pepper
¼ teaspoon salt
1½ cups frozen egg substitute, thawed
½ cup (2 ounces) shredded reduced-fat sharp
    Cheddar cheese
Green onions (optional)

Cook chopped potato in a saucepan in boiling water to cover 10 to 12 minutes or until tender. Drain well.

Coat a large nonstick skillet with cooking spray; place over medium-high heat until hot. Add potato, tomato, and next 3 ingredients; sauté until onion is tender. Pour egg substitute over vegetable mixture.

Cover skillet; cook over medium-low heat 15 minutes or until set. Sprinkle with cheese. Cover; cook 2 minutes or until cheese melts. Cut into 6 wedges, and serve immediately. Garnish with green onions, if desired. Yield: 6 servings.

PER SERVING: 100 CALORIES (19% FROM FAT)
FAT 2.1G (SATURATED FAT 1.1G)
PROTEIN 10.1G   CARBOHYDRATE 10.5G
CHOLESTEROL 6MG   SODIUM 263MG

Cheddar Potato Frittata, Garden Greens Salad, Melon with Sweet Onion Dressing,
and Zucchini-Orange Bread

GARDEN GREENS SALAD

1 large sweet red pepper
3 tablespoons white wine vinegar
2 tablespoons water
2 teaspoons olive oil
¼ teaspoon salt
⅛ teaspoon ground red pepper
1 tablespoon minced fresh basil
2 cups torn red leaf lettuce
2 cups torn green leaf lettuce
2 cups torn romaine lettuce
1 cup chopped tomato
1 cup chopped cucumber

Cut pepper in half lengthwise; remove and discard seeds and membrane. Place pepper, skin side up, on a foil-lined baking sheet. Bake at 425° for 20 to 25 minutes or until skin is browned. Cover with aluminum foil; let cool. Peel and discard skin.

Place roasted pepper, vinegar, and next 4 ingredients in container of an electric blender. Cover and process until mixture is smooth; transfer to a small bowl. Stir in basil. Cover and chill at least 1 hour.

Combine lettuces, tomato, and cucumber in a large bowl; toss gently. Arrange lettuce mixture evenly on individual plates. Spoon red pepper mixture over salads. Yield: 6 (1-cup) servings.

PER SERVING: 38 CALORIES (45% FROM FAT)
FAT 1.9G (SATURATED FAT 0.3G)
PROTEIN 1.2G CARBOHYDRATE 5.0G
CHOLESTEROL 0MG SODIUM 106MG

MELON WITH SWEET ONION DRESSING

2 cups cantaloupe balls
2 cups honeydew melon balls
2 cups watermelon balls
¼ cup sugar
¼ cup unsweetened orange juice
1 tablespoon minced onion
2 teaspoons vegetable oil
¾ teaspoon poppy seeds
¼ teaspoon salt
¼ teaspoon dry mustard

Place melon balls in a large bowl; set aside. Combine sugar and next 6 ingredients in a small jar; cover tightly, and shake vigorously. Pour orange juice mixture over melon balls, and toss gently. Cover and chill. Toss before serving. Serve with a slotted spoon. Yield: 6 (1-cup) servings.

PER SERVING: 121 CALORIES (17% FROM FAT)
FAT 2.3G (SATURATED FAT 0.6G)
PROTEIN 1.5G CARBOHYDRATE 25.8G
CHOLESTEROL 0MG SODIUM 112MG

ZUCCHINI-ORANGE BREAD

1 cup finely shredded zucchini
1¾ cups all-purpose flour
2½ teaspoons baking powder
¼ teaspoon salt
½ cup sugar
1 teaspoon grated orange rind
½ cup unsweetened orange juice
⅓ cup frozen egg substitute, thawed
2 tablespoons vegetable oil
½ teaspoon orange extract
Vegetable cooking spray

Press zucchini between paper towels to remove excess moisture. Combine zucchini, flour, and next 4 ingredients in a large bowl. Combine orange juice, egg substitute, oil, and orange extract, stirring well. Add to dry ingredients, stirring just until dry ingredients are moistened.

Spoon batter into an 8½- x 4½- x 3-inch loafpan coated with cooking spray. Bake at 375° for 40 to 45 minutes or until a wooden pick inserted in center comes out clean. Let cool in pan 10 minutes; remove from pan, and let cool completely on a wire rack. Yield: 16 (½-inch) slices.

PER SLICE: 98 CALORIES (17% FROM FAT)
FAT 1.9G (SATURATED FAT 0.3G)
PROTEIN 2.1G CARBOHYDRATE 18.1G
CHOLESTEROL 0MG SODIUM 45MG

RUSTIC ITALIAN SUPPER

After a busy weekday, relax with a casual Italian meal of soup and biscuits. This simple meatless dinner can be on the table in less than 45 minutes. First get the soup started, and then prepare the dough for the biscuits. After you put the biscuits in the oven to bake, add pasta to the soup mixture.

If you want to end the meal with dessert, whip the Amaretto Velvet Frosty in a blender right before serving.

Italian Pasta and Bean Soup

Sage and Cheese Biscuits

Amaretto Velvet Frosty

Serves 8
TOTAL CALORIES PER SERVING: 518
(CALORIES FROM FAT: 15%)

ITALIAN PASTA AND BEAN SOUP

Vegetable cooking spray
1 tablespoon olive oil
1 cup chopped onion
1 cup sliced carrot
½ cup chopped green pepper
2 cloves garlic, crushed
1 (14½-ounce) can vegetable or chicken broth
1¾ cups water
1 (28-ounce) can crushed tomatoes
1 (15-ounce) can cannellini beans, rinsed and drained
1 (15-ounce) can red kidney beans, rinsed and drained
1½ teaspoons dried Italian seasoning
½ teaspoon hot sauce
¼ teaspoon pepper
6 ounces ditalini (small tubular pasta), uncooked
½ cup freshly grated Parmesan cheese

Coat a Dutch oven with cooking spray; add oil and place over medium-high heat. Add onion and next 3 ingredients; sauté until vegetables are crisp-tender.

Add vegetable broth and next 7 ingredients; bring to a boil. Reduce heat to low; cover and simmer 20 minutes, stirring occasionally.

Add pasta to vegetable mixture. Cover and cook 10 to 15 minutes or until pasta is tender. Ladle soup into individual bowls; top each serving with 1 tablespoon cheese. Yield: 8 (1¼-cup) servings.

Note: Cannellini beans are white kidney beans. You can use any other small white beans or an additional can of red kidney beans if you don't have cannellini beans in the pantry.

PER SERVING: 244 CALORIES (17% FROM FAT)
FAT 4.7G (SATURATED FAT 1.5G)
PROTEIN 12.1G   CARBOHYDRATE 39.2G
CHOLESTEROL 5MG   SODIUM 601MG

Italian Pasta and Bean Soup (recipe on page 15) and Sage and Cheese Biscuits

SAGE AND CHEESE BISCUITS

1 cup all-purpose flour
1½ teaspoons baking powder
¼ teaspoon salt
1 teaspoon ground sage
½ teaspoon sugar
⅛ teaspoon freshly ground pepper
2 tablespoons stick margarine
¼ cup plus 2 tablespoons evaporated skimmed milk
2 tablespoons (½ ounce) shredded reduced-fat Monterey Jack cheese
1½ teaspoons all-purpose flour

Combine first 6 ingredients in a large bowl; cut in margarine with a pastry blender until mixture resembles coarse meal.

Add milk and cheese, stirring just until dry ingredients are moistened.

Sprinkle 1½ teaspoons flour evenly over work surface. Turn dough out onto floured surface, and knead 10 to 12 times. Roll dough to ½-inch thickness; cut into rounds, using a 2-inch biscuit cutter.

Place rounds on an ungreased baking sheet. Bake at 450° for 8 to 10 minutes or until biscuits are golden. Yield: 8 biscuits.

PER BISCUIT: 99 CALORIES (31% FROM FAT)
FAT 3.4G (SATURATED FAT 0.8G)
PROTEIN 3.0G CARBOHYDRATE 14.1G
CHOLESTEROL 2MG SODIUM 130MG

AMARETTO VELVET FROSTY

2 cups skim milk
¼ cup instant nonfat dry milk powder
¾ cup amaretto
3 cups vanilla nonfat yogurt
¼ teaspoon vanilla extract
⅛ teaspoon almond extract
Ice cubes
1 tablespoon chopped almonds, toasted and divided

Combine skim milk and nonfat dry milk powder, stirring well. Add amaretto and next 3 ingredients. Place half of milk mixture in container of an electric blender.

Gradually add enough ice cubes to bring mixture to a 4-cup level; cover and process until smooth. Pour mixture into a large pitcher. Repeat procedure with the remaining half of milk mixture. Stir well. Sprinkle each serving evenly with almonds. Serve immediately. Yield: 8 (1-cup) servings.

PER SERVING: 175 CALORIES (4% FROM FAT)
FAT 0.7G (SATURATED FAT 0.2G)
PROTEIN 6.2G CARBOHYDRATE 25.3G
CHOLESTEROL 2MG SODIUM 97MG

Amaretto Velvet Frosty

Unsloppy Joes and Festival Slaw

GAME NIGHT SPECIAL

Here's a fun meatless menu to serve for an old-fashioned family game night! Even the pickiest of eaters will enjoy the vegetable-packed sandwiches called Unsloppy Joes. The hearty sandwich filling and slaw can both be made ahead of time. Then assemble the ingredients for Maple Bread Pudding so that the mixture can chill for 40 minutes before baking.

Now let the games begin!

Unsloppy Joes

Festival Slaw

Maple Bread Pudding

Serves 8
TOTAL CALORIES PER SERVING: 350
(CALORIES FROM FAT: 14%)

UNSLOPPY JOES

Vegetable cooking spray
½ cup chopped onion
½ cup chopped celery
½ cup diced carrot
½ cup diced green pepper
1 clove garlic, minced
1 (14½-ounce) can no-salt-added whole
    tomatoes, undrained and crushed
1½ tablespoons chili powder
1 tablespoon no-salt-added tomato paste
1 tablespoon vinegar
1 teaspoon pepper
1 (15½-ounce) can red kidney beans, drained
8 (2½-ounce) kaiser rolls

Coat a large nonstick skillet with cooking spray; place over medium-high heat until hot. Add onion, celery, carrot, green pepper, and garlic; sauté until tender. Stir in crushed tomato and next 4 ingredients. Cover, reduce heat, and simmer 10 minutes. Add kidney beans, and cook an additional 5 minutes or until thoroughly heated.

Cut a ¼-inch slice off top of each kaiser roll; set aside. Hollow out center of rolls, leaving ½-inch-thick shells; reserve inside of rolls for other uses. Spoon bean mixture evenly into rolls; top with slices. Serve immediately. Yield: 8 servings.

PER SERVING: 135 CALORIES (12% FROM FAT)
FAT 1.8G (SATURATED FAT 0.4G)
PROTEIN 5.9G CARBOHYDRATE 25.0G
CHOLESTEROL 0MG SODIUM 279MG

FESTIVAL SLAW

3 cups shredded cabbage
1 cup shredded red cabbage
1 cup shredded carrot
¼ cup finely chopped onion
¼ cup chopped dry roasted cashews
¼ cup white wine vinegar
¼ cup unsweetened pineapple juice
1 tablespoon Dijon mustard
⅛ teaspoon salt
⅛ teaspoon pepper

Combine cabbage, red cabbage, carrot, onion, and cashews in a medium bowl; toss gently.

Combine vinegar and next 4 ingredients; stir well. Add to cabbage mixture, and toss gently. Cover and chill thoroughly. Yield: 8 (½-cup) servings.

PER SERVING: 43 CALORIES (40% FROM FAT)
FAT 1.9G (SATURATED FAT 0.3G)
PROTEIN 1.1G CARBOHYDRATE 5.8G
CHOLESTEROL 0MG SODIUM 124MG

MAPLE BREAD PUDDING

6 ounces Italian bread, cut into 1-inch cubes
    (about 3½ cups)
Vegetable cooking spray
2½ cups 1% low-fat milk
⅓ cup maple syrup
2 tablespoons sugar
1 teaspoon vanilla extract
½ teaspoon ground cinnamon
⅛ teaspoon salt
⅛ teaspoon ground nutmeg
2 egg whites
1 egg
⅓ cup raisins

Arrange bread cubes in a single layer on a baking sheet. Bake at 325° for 10 minutes. Place bread cubes in an 8-inch square baking dish coated with cooking spray.

Combine milk and next 8 ingredients in a medium bowl, and stir with a wire whisk until well-blended. Stir in raisins. Pour milk mixture over bread, tossing gently to coat. Cover and chill 40 minutes.

Bake at 350° for 1 hour and 15 minutes or until pudding is set. Serve warm. Yield: 8 servings.

PER SERVING: 172 CALORIES (9% FROM FAT)
FAT 1.7G (SATURATED FAT 0.7G)
PROTEIN 6.3G CARBOHYDRATE 32.8G
CHOLESTEROL 30MG SODIUM 223MG

SALAD BAR SUPPER
(pictured on page 10)

Stopping by the salad bar of the local supermarket has become a popular and convenient way to pick up a quick meal. You get the goodness of fresh fruits and vegetables without having to spend time chopping and cutting.

For a change of pace, use the variety of salad fixings from the supermarket to create a satisfying pasta supper. Gazpacho Pasta is made by sautéing vegetables that are commonly featured in salad bars and tossing those vegetables with spaghetti.

Even the spinach and strawberries for Ginger-Berry Tossed Salad and the cantaloupe for dessert are available from many salad bars. Then round out this quick-fix meal with Tangy French Bread.

Gazpacho Pasta

Ginger-Berry Tossed Salad

Tangy French Bread

Sparkling Cantaloupe Sherbet

Serves 6
TOTAL CALORIES PER SERVING: 427
(CALORIES FROM FAT: 18%)

GAZPACHO PASTA

6 ounces spaghetti, uncooked
Vegetable cooking spray
1 cup broccoli flowerets
1 cup thinly sliced carrots
1 cup sliced zucchini
¼ cup sliced onion
1 small sweet yellow pepper, cut into thin strips
½ cup sliced cucumber
½ cup sliced fresh mushrooms
1 small tomato, cut into 8 wedges
2 tablespoons dry vermouth
¼ cup plus 2 tablespoons grated Parmesan cheese
1 tablespoon minced fresh parsley
¼ teaspoon sweet red pepper flakes

Cook pasta according to package directions, omitting salt and fat. Drain and set aside.

Coat a large nonstick skillet with cooking spray; place over medium heat until hot. Add broccoli and next 3 ingredients; sauté 4 minutes. Add pepper strips, cucumber, and mushrooms; sauté 4 minutes. Add pasta, tomato, and vermouth; toss gently. Cook until thoroughly heated. Sprinkle with cheese, parsley, and pepper flakes; toss gently. Serve immediately. Yield: 6 (1-cup) servings.

PER SERVING: 155 CALORIES (13% FROM FAT)
FAT 2.3G (SATURATED FAT 1.1G)
PROTEIN 7.0G CARBOHYDRATE 26.9G
CHOLESTEROL 4MG SODIUM 109MG

GINGER-BERRY TOSSED SALAD

1 cup sliced fresh strawberries
½ cup 1% low-fat cottage cheese
½ teaspoon ground ginger
3 cups torn fresh spinach
3 cups torn iceberg lettuce
½ cup sliced celery
¼ cup unsalted sunflower kernels

Combine first 3 ingredients in container of an electric blender or food processor; cover and process until smooth. Chill.

Place torn spinach, lettuce, and celery in a large bowl, tossing gently to combine. Divide spinach mixture among 6 individual plates. Pour dressing mixture over spinach mixture; sprinkle with sunflower kernels. Yield: 6 servings.

PER SERVING: 66 CALORIES (46% FROM FAT)
FAT 3.4G (SATURATED FAT 0.5G)
PROTEIN 5.0G CARBOHYDRATE 5.2G
CHOLESTEROL 1MG SODIUM 110MG

TANGY FRENCH BREAD

6 (1-ounce) slices French bread, toasted
2 tablespoons commercial reduced-calorie
    Italian dressing
½ cup (2 ounces) shredded part-skim
    mozzarella cheese
1 tablespoon minced fresh parsley
2 teaspoons minced fresh basil

Place bread slices on a broiler rack. Brush top side of each bread slice lightly with salad dressing. Sprinkle cheese, parsley, and basil evenly over bread slices. Broil 5½ inches from heat (with electric oven door partially opened) until cheese melts. Serve immediately. Yield: 6 servings.

PER SERVING: 109 CALORIES (18% FROM FAT)
FAT 2.2G (SATURATED FAT 1.2G)
PROTEIN 4.9G CARBOHYDRATE 16.3G
CHOLESTEROL 6MG SODIUM 280MG

SPARKLING CANTALOUPE SHERBET

3 cups cubed cantaloupe
1 (10-ounce) bottle lemon-lime flavored
    sparkling mineral water, chilled
2 cups lime sherbet
Fresh mint sprigs (optional)

Combine cantaloupe and mineral water in a bowl; toss gently. Spoon ½ cup cantaloupe into individual dessert dishes using a slotted spoon; reserve water. Top each serving with ⅓ cup of sherbet. Spoon remaining mineral water evenly over sherbet. Garnish with fresh mint sprigs, if desired. Serve immediately. Yield: 6 servings.

PER SERVING: 97 CALORIES (7% FROM FAT)
FAT 0.8G (SATURATED FAT 0.1G)
PROTEIN 1.3G CARBOHYDRATE 22.5G
CHOLESTEROL 0MG SODIUM 52MG

FYI

Health experts tell us that the best sources of vitamins and minerals are actual foods rather than supplements. That's welcome news for vegetarians, who eat large amounts of vitamin-rich vegetables, fruit, and grains. Along with the major vitamins, such as vitamins A and C, these foods provide valuable fiber and trace vitamins and minerals.

The daily food guide on page 8 shows what amounts of specific foods are needed to provide adequate vitamins and minerals. If you think that you need a vitamin or mineral supplement, check with your doctor or registered dietitian.

SUMMERTIME HARVEST

Take advantage of summer's fresh produce with this menu that boasts only 13 percent of calories from fat. The squash casserole is high enough in protein to be considered the main dish. Lemon Green Beans, Country Corncakes, and three new potatoes boost the complex carbohydrates.

Summer Squash Casserole

Lemon Green Beans

Boiled new potatoes

Country Corncakes

Fresh berries

Serves 4
TOTAL CALORIES PER SERVING: 482
(CALORIES FROM FAT: 13%)

Lemon Green Beans and Country Corncakes

SUMMER SQUASH CASSEROLE

2 pounds yellow squash, sliced
⅔ cup chopped onion
¼ cup plus 2 tablespoons chopped green
 pepper
⅔ cup (2.7 ounces) shredded reduced-fat
 Cheddar cheese
½ cup frozen egg substitute, thawed
1 (4-ounce) jar diced pimiento, drained
¼ teaspoon salt
¼ teaspoon pepper
Vegetable cooking spray
3 tablespoons fine, dry breadcrumbs
2 tablespoons chopped fresh parsley
⅛ teaspoon paprika

Place squash, onion, and green pepper in a vegetable steamer over boiling water; cover and steam 10 to 12 minutes or until vegetables are crisp-tender. Combine steamed vegetables, cheese, and next 4 ingredients in a medium bowl; stir gently. Spoon mixture into a 2-quart baking dish coated with cooking spray.

Combine breadcrumbs, parsley, and paprika, stirring well; sprinkle over squash mixture. Bake at 350° for 25 to 30 minutes or until thoroughly heated. Yield: 4 (1-cup) servings.

PER SERVING: 156 CALORIES (27% FROM FAT)
FAT 4.6G (SATURATED FAT 2.2G)
PROTEIN 12.5G CARBOHYDRATE 18.7G
CHOLESTEROL 12MG SODIUM 381MG

LEMON GREEN BEANS

½ pound fresh green beans
½ small sweet red pepper, cut crosswise into
 rings
¼ teaspoon dried basil
1 tablespoon lemon rind strips
1 tablespoon lemon juice
1 teaspoon sesame seeds, toasted

Wash beans; trim ends, and remove strings. Cut beans into 2-inch pieces. Combine beans, pepper rings, and basil in a medium saucepan with a small amount of water. Bring to a boil. Cover, reduce heat, and simmer 12 to 15 minutes or until vegetables are tender. Drain well. Transfer mixture to a serving bowl. Add lemon rind, lemon juice, and sesame seeds; toss. Yield: 4 (½-cup) servings.

PER SERVING: 25 CALORIES (18% FROM FAT)
FAT 0.5G (SATURATED FAT 0.1G)
PROTEIN 1.3G CARBOHYDRATE 5.2G
CHOLESTEROL 0MG SODIUM 4MG

COUNTRY CORNCAKES

1 cup fresh corn cut from the cob (about 2
 ears)
½ cup yellow cornmeal
1 cup boiling water
2 teaspoons honey
¼ teaspoon salt
2 egg whites
Vegetable cooking spray

Cook corn, covered, in boiling water to cover 8 to 10 minutes or until tender; drain corn, and set aside to cool.

Combine corn, cornmeal, and next 3 ingredients in a medium bowl; stir well.

Beat egg whites at high speed of an electric mixer until stiff peaks form. (Do not overbeat.) Fold egg whites into corn mixture.

Pour ¼ cup batter onto a hot griddle coated with cooking spray. Cook 3 minutes on each side or until brown. Yield: 12 (3½-inch) corncakes.

PER SERVING: 40 CALORIES (7% FROM FAT)
FAT 0.3G (SATURATED FAT 0.0G)
PROTEIN 1.5G CARBOHYDRATE 8.2G
CHOLESTEROL 0MG SODIUM 59MG

Farmer's Market Vegetable Bowl (recipe on page 28)

MORNING ENTRÉES

*M*ost of us eat our share of bagels, toast, and cereal on busy mornings. But when you have a few extra minutes, try a recipe from this collection of meatless breakfast dishes—from jazzed-up scrambled eggs (made with egg substitute) to a company-perfect strata. Each is considered hearty enough to be a breakfast main dish, offering 7 or more grams of protein per serving.

One of the best ways to start the day without meat is to feast on pancakes or waffles. A stack of Buttermilk Pancakes with Orange Syrup (page 44) provides 10 grams of protein along with plenty of complex carbohydrates.

EGG SUBSTITUTE

8 egg whites
⅓ cup instant nonfat dry milk powder
2 tablespoons water
2 teaspoons vegetable oil
3 drops yellow food coloring (optional)

Combine all ingredients in container of an electric blender or food processor; cover and process 30 seconds.

To store, refrigerate mixture in a covered container up to 1 week, or freeze in an airtight container up to 1 month. Yield: 4 (¼-cup) servings.

PER SERVING: 88 CALORIES (24% FROM FAT)
FAT 2.3G (SATURATED FAT 0.5G)
PROTEIN 10.3G   CARBOHYDRATE 5.9G
CHOLESTEROL 2MG   SODIUM 158MG

BAKED EGG CUPS

4 (1-ounce) slices whole wheat bread
Vegetable cooking spray
1 tablespoon grated Parmesan cheese
⅛ teaspoon garlic powder
⅛ teaspoon ground red pepper
1 cup frozen egg substitute, thawed

Trim crust from bread; reserve for other uses. Press 1 slice into each of 4 (6-ounce) custard cups coated with cooking spray. Bake at 425° for 8 minutes.

Combine cheese, garlic powder, and pepper; stir well. Pour ¼ cup egg substitute into each cup; sprinkle with cheese mixture. Bake at 350° for 15 to 17 minutes or until set. Serve immediately. Yield: 4 servings.

PER SERVING: 81 CALORIES (12% FROM FAT)
FAT 1.1G (SATURATED FAT 0.3G)
PROTEIN 8.4G   CARBOHYDRATE 9.6G
CHOLESTEROL 2MG   SODIUM 207MG

SUNSHINE SCRAMBLE

1 cup frozen egg substitute, thawed
¼ cup skim milk
¼ cup nonfat sour cream
¼ teaspoon salt
⅛ teaspoon pepper
¼ cup chopped green onions
Vegetable cooking spray

Combine first 5 ingredients in container of an electric blender or food processor; cover and process 10 seconds or until frothy. Transfer mixture to a medium bowl; stir in green onions.

Coat a large nonstick skillet with cooking spray; place over medium heat until hot. Add egg substitute mixture; cook, stirring frequently, until mixture is firm but still moist. Yield: 4 servings.

PER SERVING: 48 CALORIES (4% FROM FAT)
FAT 0.2G (SATURATED FAT 0.0G)
PROTEIN 7.6G   CARBOHYDRATE 3.0G
CHOLESTEROL 0MG   SODIUM 255MG

JALAPEÑO BRUNCH SCRAMBLE

4 (6-inch) corn tortillas
Vegetable cooking spray
¾ cup sliced green onions
½ cup diced sweet red pepper
¼ cup sliced jalapeño pepper
¼ cup minced fresh cilantro
1 teaspoon ground cumin
2 cups frozen egg substitute, thawed
⅓ cup skim milk
¼ teaspoon ground red pepper
⅛ teaspoon salt
¼ cup (2 ounces) crumbled feta cheese

Fill a shallow baking dish with water. Dip tortillas, one at a time, into water for 2 seconds. Drain; place on an ungreased baking sheet. Bake at 500° for 4 minutes. Turn; bake 2 minutes or until crisp. Set aside.

Jalapeño Brunch Scramble

Coat a large nonstick skillet with cooking spray; place over medium-high heat until hot. Add green onions, sweet red pepper, and jalapeño pepper; sauté until tender. Transfer to a bowl; stir in cilantro and cumin. Wipe skillet dry with a paper towel.

Combine egg substitute, milk, ground red pepper, and salt; stir well. Crumble tortillas into egg mixture; let stand 5 minutes.

Coat skillet with cooking spray; place over medium heat until hot enough to sizzle a drop of water. Pour egg substitute mixture into skillet. As the mixture begins to cook, gently lift edges with a spatula, and tilt pan to allow uncooked portions to flow underneath. When egg mixture is set, spoon vegetable mixture over top, and sprinkle with cheese. Broil 5½ inches from heat (with electric oven door partially opened) 1 minute or until cheese softens. Yield: 4 servings.

PER SERVING: 191 CALORIES (23% FROM FAT)
FAT 4.8G (SATURATED FAT 2.3G)
PROTEIN 17.5G CARBOHYDRATE 19.8G
CHOLESTEROL 13MG   SODIUM 480MG

FARMER'S MARKET VEGETABLE BOWL

(pictured on page 24)

2 small sweet red peppers
Vegetable cooking spray
2 teaspoons olive oil, divided
2 cups sliced zucchini
1 small onion, sliced
½ cup thinly sliced carrot
2 cloves garlic, crushed
12 cherry tomatoes, halved
1½ tablespoons minced fresh basil
1 cup frozen egg substitute, thawed
⅔ cup all-purpose flour
½ cup skim milk
¼ teaspoon salt
½ cup (2 ounces) crumbled feta cheese

Cut sweet red peppers in half lengthwise; remove and discard seeds and membranes. Place peppers, skin side up, on a large baking sheet; flatten with palm of hand. Broil 5½ inches from heat (with electric oven door partially opened) 12 minutes or until charred. Place peppers in ice water; chill 5 minutes. Remove from water; peel and discard skins. Cut into thin strips, and set aside.

Coat a large nonstick skillet with cooking spray; add 1 teaspoon olive oil. Place over medium-high heat until hot. Add zucchini, onion, carrot, and garlic; sauté 10 to 12 minutes or until vegetables are tender. Stir in peppers, tomatoes, and basil. Remove from heat, and keep warm.

Combine egg substitute, flour, milk, and salt in a medium bowl; beat with a wire whisk until smooth.

Coat a 9-inch cast-iron skillet with cooking spray; brush with remaining 1 teaspoon olive oil. Place skillet in a 450° oven for 4 minutes or until hot. Pour batter into skillet. Bake at 450° for 15 minutes. Reduce heat to 375°, and bake 15 minutes or until puffed and browned.

Spoon vegetable mixture into shell; sprinkle with feta cheese. Serve immediately. Yield: 4 servings.

PER SERVING: 224 CALORIES (25% FROM FAT)
FAT 6.3G (SATURATED FAT 2.6G)
PROTEIN 13.4G CARBOHYDRATE 29.5G
CHOLESTEROL 13MG   SODIUM 426MG

EGGS SARDOU

Vegetable cooking spray
¼ cup chopped green onions
1 (9-ounce) package frozen artichoke hearts, thawed
4 cups tightly packed torn spinach leaves
2 hard-cooked eggs, peeled and sliced
1½ tablespoons all-purpose flour
1 cup skim milk
2 tablespoons grated Parmesan cheese, divided
⅛ teaspoon dried thyme
⅛ teaspoon freshly ground pepper
1 tablespoon plus 1 teaspoon lemon juice
⅛ teaspoon paprika
¼ cup nonfat sour cream

Coat a large nonstick skillet with cooking spray; place over medium heat until hot. Add green onions and artichokes; sauté 5 minutes. Remove from heat; stir in spinach. Divide spinach mixture evenly between 2 individual baking dishes coated with cooking spray. Arrange egg over spinach mixture; set aside.

Place flour in a small saucepan; gradually add milk, stirring with a wire whisk until blended. Place over medium heat, and cook 5 minutes or until thickened, stirring constantly. Remove from heat; stir in 1 tablespoon cheese, thyme, pepper, and lemon juice.

Pour ½ cup sauce over each serving. Combine remaining 1 tablespoon cheese and paprika; sprinkle over each serving. Place dishes on a baking sheet. Cover with aluminum foil, and bake at 350° for 20 minutes. To serve, top each dish with 2 tablespoons sour cream. Yield: 2 servings.

PER SERVING: 272 CALORIES (30% FROM FAT)
FAT 9.0G (SATURATED FAT 3.0G)
PROTEIN 22.0G CARBOHYDRATE 28.6G
CHOLESTEROL 219MG   SODIUM 390MG

Eggs Sardou

Huevos Rancheros with Pita Chips

HUEVOS RANCHEROS WITH PITA CHIPS

1 (8-inch) pita bread round
Butter-flavored vegetable cooking spray
½ teaspoon dried basil
½ teaspoon garlic powder
½ teaspoon ground cumin
1 (16-ounce) can red beans, drained
1 (14½-ounce) can Mexican-style stewed
    tomatoes
2 tablespoons sliced green onions
4 eggs
¼ cup commercial no-salt-added salsa
¼ cup nonfat sour cream
Fresh cilantro sprigs (optional)

Separate pita bread into 2 rounds; cut each round into 8 wedges. Place wedges on an ungreased baking sheet; coat with cooking spray. Combine basil, garlic powder, and cumin; sprinkle over wedges. Bake at 400° for 5 minutes or until crisp and lightly browned. Remove chips from baking sheet; let cool completely on a wire rack.

Combine beans, tomatoes, and sliced green onions in a saucepan. Cook, uncovered, over medium heat 10 minutes, stirring occasionally. Set aside, and keep warm.

Add water to a large saucepan to a depth of 2 inches. Bring to a boil; reduce heat, and maintain at a light simmer. Break eggs, one at a time, into water. Simmer 7 to 9 minutes or until internal temperature of egg reaches 160°. Remove eggs with a slotted spoon.

To serve, arrange 4 pita wedges around edge of each individual serving plate; top evenly with bean mixture. Top each serving with an egg. Spoon 1 tablespoon salsa and 1 tablespoon sour cream over each serving. Garnish each with a cilantro sprig, if desired. Serve immediately. Yield: 4 servings.

PER SERVING: 265 CALORIES (22% FROM FAT)
FAT 6.4G (SATURATED FAT 1.7G)
PROTEIN 16.2G   CARBOHYDRATE 35.1G
CHOLESTEROL 221MG   SODIUM 594MG

SQUASH AND POTATO FRITTATA

A frittata is a round, open-faced Italian omelet that is cooked over low heat.

¾ pound unpeeled round red potatoes (about
    9 small)
Vegetable cooking spray
1 cup thinly sliced zucchini
1 cup thinly sliced yellow squash
¼ cup loosely packed fresh parsley
½ teaspoon grated lemon rind
¼ teaspoon salt
¼ teaspoon ground pepper
1 clove garlic, crushed
2 teaspoons olive oil
½ cup (2 ounces) crumbled feta cheese
1½ cups frozen egg substitute, thawed

Place potatoes in a medium saucepan; cover with water, and bring to a boil over medium-high heat. Cook, uncovered, 20 minutes or just until tender. Drain; let cool. Peel potatoes, and cut into ¼-inch slices.

Coat a large nonstick skillet with cooking spray; place over low heat until hot. Add zucchini and yellow squash. Cover and cook 10 minutes or until tender. Combine squash mixture, parsley, and next 4 ingredients in a bowl; toss gently.

Wipe skillet with paper towels. Heat oil in skillet over medium heat. Arrange potato slices in bottom of skillet, overlapping slices. Cook over medium heat, without turning, 10 minutes or until potato slices begin to brown. Spoon half of the squash mixture evenly over the potato layer; top first with feta cheese and then with the remaining squash mixture.

Pour egg substitute over vegetable mixture; cover and cook over medium-low heat 20 minutes or until set. Serve warm. Yield: 4 servings.

PER SERVING: 168 CALORIES (30% FROM FAT)
FAT 5.6G (SATURATED FAT 2.5G)
PROTEIN 13.3G   CARBOHYDRATE 16.5G
CHOLESTEROL 13MG   SODIUM 447MG

FRITTATA VERDE

¾ ounce dried porcini mushrooms
2 cups water
1 pound fresh spinach
2 eggs
3 egg whites
3 tablespoons grated Parmesan cheese, divided
2 tablespoons dry white wine
1 tablespoon thinly sliced green onions
¼ teaspoon black pepper
⅛ teaspoon salt
⅛ teaspoon ground nutmeg
⅛ teaspoon ground red pepper
Vegetable cooking spray
1 cup finely chopped onion
1 large clove garlic, minced
½ teaspoon dried basil
¼ teaspoon dried oregano

Combine dried mushrooms and 2 cups water in a saucepan, and bring to a boil; remove from heat. Cover and let stand 30 minutes. Drain; chop mushrooms, and set aside.

Remove stems from spinach, and wash leaves. Place spinach in a large Dutch oven; cover with water, and bring to a boil. Cover, reduce heat, and simmer 10 minutes; drain well. Finely chop spinach, and set aside.

Combine eggs and egg whites in a large bowl; stir with a wire whisk. Stir in spinach, 2 tablespoons cheese, wine, and next 5 ingredients; set aside.

Coat an 8-inch nonstick skillet with cooking spray; place over medium heat until hot. Add onion; sauté 3 minutes. Add garlic; sauté 1 minute. Add mushrooms, basil, and oregano; sauté 1 minute. Stir onion mixture into spinach mixture.

Recoat skillet with cooking spray. Pour spinach mixture into skillet, and place over medium-low heat; cover and cook 12 minutes or until almost set.

Top with remaining 1 tablespoon cheese. Wrap handle of skillet with foil, and broil 6 inches from heat (with electric oven door partially opened) 3 minutes or until cheese melts. Yield: 4 servings.

PER SERVING: 135 CALORIES (30% FROM FAT)
FAT 4.5G (SATURATED FAT 1.6G)
PROTEIN 11.7G   CARBOHYDRATE 13.0G
CHOLESTEROL 109MG   SODIUM 308MG

SPINACH-HERB OMELET

1 cup seeded, chopped unpeeled tomato
1 teaspoon chopped fresh dill
1 teaspoon minced fresh chives
Dash of salt
Vegetable cooking spray
¼ cup chopped purple onion
2 cups loosely packed chopped fresh spinach
¾ cup cooked rice (cooked without salt or fat)
3 tablespoons (¾ ounce) crumbled feta cheese
1 tablespoon chopped fresh dill, divided
1 tablespoon minced fresh chives, divided
2 egg yolks
1 tablespoon skim milk
3 egg whites
Dash of salt
1 tablespoon all-purpose flour
⅛ teaspoon freshly ground pepper
Fresh dill sprigs (optional)

Combine first 4 ingredients; stir well, and set aside. Coat a nonstick skillet with cooking spray; place over medium-high heat until hot. Add onion, and sauté 2 minutes. Add spinach, and sauté 1½ minutes or until spinach begins to wilt. Stir in rice, cheese, 1½ teaspoons dill, and 1½ teaspoons chives, and set aside.

Beat egg yolks in a bowl until thick and pale (about 5 minutes). Add milk; beat until blended, and set aside.

Beat egg whites and salt until soft peaks form. Add remaining 1½ teaspoons dill, remaining 1½ teaspoons chives, flour, and pepper, beating until stiff peaks form. Gently fold into egg yolk mixture.

Coat a medium nonstick skillet with cooking spray, and place over medium heat until hot. Spread egg mixture evenly in skillet; top with spinach mixture. Cover, reduce heat to medium-low, and cook 10 minutes or until center is set.

Carefully loosen omelet with a spatula, and fold in half; gently slide onto a warm serving plate. Spoon tomato mixture over top. Cut omelet in half; garnish with dill, if desired. Yield: 2 servings.

PER SERVING: 262 CALORIES (31% FROM FAT)
FAT 8.9G (SATURATED FAT 3.3G)
PROTEIN 14.5G   CARBOHYDRATE 31.8G
CHOLESTEROL 228MG   SODIUM 410MG

Spinach-Herb Omelet

OMELET FOR ONE

¼ cup julienne-sliced carrot
¼ cup julienne-sliced zucchini
1½ teaspoons chopped fresh chives
¾ teaspoon chopped fresh dill
2 tablespoons part-skim ricotta cheese
2 tablespoons nonfat sour cream
½ cup frozen egg substitute, thawed
2 teaspoons water
⅛ teaspoon salt
Vegetable cooking spray

Arrange carrot and zucchini in a vegetable steamer over boiling water. Cover and steam 2 to 3 minutes or until crisp-tender; drain well.

Combine steamed vegetables, chives, and next 3 ingredients in a bowl; stir well. Set aside. Combine egg substitute, water, and salt in a bowl; stir well.

Coat a small nonstick skillet with cooking spray; place over medium heat until hot. Pour egg substitute mixture into skillet. As mixture begins to cook, gently lift edges of omelet with a spatula, and tilt pan to allow uncooked portion to flow underneath. When set, spoon vegetable mixture over half of omelet. Loosen omelet with a spatula, and carefully fold in half. Slide onto a plate. Yield: 1 serving.

PER SERVING: 143 CALORIES (18% FROM FAT)
FAT 2.8G (SATURATED FAT 1.5G)
PROTEIN 18.3G CARBOHYDRATE 9.8G
CHOLESTEROL 10MG SODIUM 543MG

GARDEN-FRESH OMELET

½ cup frozen egg substitute, thawed
2 tablespoons skim milk
1½ teaspoons minced fresh dill
⅛ teaspoon pepper
4 egg whites
1 tablespoon all-purpose flour
Vegetable cooking spray
½ cup alfalfa sprouts
1 medium tomato, thinly sliced
1½ tablespoons grated Parmesan cheese

Combine first 4 ingredients in a small bowl; stir well, and set aside.

Beat egg whites at high speed of an electric mixer until soft peaks form; add flour, beating until stiff peaks form. Fold egg white mixture into egg substitute mixture.

Coat a small nonstick skillet with cooking spray; place over medium heat until hot. Pour half of egg white mixture into skillet, spreading evenly. Cover and cook 5 minutes or until center is set. Arrange half of sprouts, tomato, and cheese over one half of omelet. Loosen omelet with a spatula, and fold in half. Slide omelet onto a warm serving plate. Repeat procedure with remaining half of egg white mixture, sprouts, tomato, and cheese. Yield: 2 servings.

PER SERVING: 122 CALORIES (12% FROM FAT)
FAT 1.7G (SATURATED FAT 0.8G)
PROTEIN 16.4G CARBOHYDRATE 10.3G
CHOLESTEROL 3MG SODIUM 283MG

ROASTED RED PEPPER AND GARLIC QUICHE

2 medium-size sweet red peppers (about 1 pound)
1 whole head garlic
Vegetable cooking spray
1 medium zucchini, halved lengthwise and thinly sliced (about 1⅓ cups)
¼ teaspoon dried basil
1 (10-ounce) can refrigerated pizza crust dough
½ cup (2 ounces) shredded provolone cheese
½ cup 1% low-fat cottage cheese
½ cup evaporated skimmed milk
2 eggs
1 tablespoon grated Parmesan cheese

Cut peppers in half lengthwise; discard seeds and membranes. Place peppers, skin side up, on a baking sheet covered with aluminum foil; flatten peppers with palm of hand. Remove papery skin of

Roasted Red Pepper and Garlic Quiche

garlic; do not peel or separate cloves. Add whole garlic to baking sheet. Bake at 500° for 30 minutes or until peppers are blackened and charred. Place peppers in a heavy-duty, zip-top plastic bag, and seal; let stand 15 minutes. Remove peppers from bag; peel and discard skins. Coarsely chop peppers; set aside. Separate garlic cloves, and squeeze to extract garlic pulp; discard skins. Set pulp aside.

Coat a small nonstick skillet with cooking spray; place over medium-high heat until hot. Add zucchini; sauté 3 minutes. Remove from heat; stir in chopped roasted peppers and basil, and set aside.

Unroll pizza crust dough; fold corners of dough toward center, and pat or roll into a 10-inch circle. Fit dough into a 9-inch pieplate coated with cooking spray; flute edges. Sprinkle provolone cheese over bottom of crust. Top with zucchini mixture; set aside.

Position knife blade in food processor bowl; add cottage cheese and garlic pulp, and process until smooth. Add milk and eggs; process 30 seconds. Pour over zucchini mixture; sprinkle with Parmesan cheese. Bake at 350° for 40 minutes or until a knife inserted 1 inch from center comes out clean; let stand 10 minutes. Yield: 6 servings.

PER SERVING: 240 CALORIES (24% FROM FAT)
FAT 6.5G (SATURATED FAT 2.5G)
PROTEIN 14.0G   CARBOHYDRATE 30.1G
CHOLESTEROL 82MG   SODIUM 451MG

Fresh Tomato and Basil Quiche

FRESH TOMATO AND BASIL QUICHE

1 (7-ounce) package refrigerated breadstick
   dough
Vegetable cooking spray
1 teaspoon olive oil
1 cup slivered onion
1 clove garlic, minced
¾ cup (3 ounces) shredded part-skim
   mozzarella cheese
1 cup (¼-inch-thick) sliced plum tomato
¼ cup shredded fresh basil
1 cup evaporated skimmed milk
1½ teaspoons cornstarch
¼ teaspoon freshly ground pepper
2 eggs
1 egg white

Unroll breadstick dough, separating into strips.
Working on a flat surface, coil one strip of dough
around itself in a spiral pattern. Add second strip of
dough to the end of the first strip, pinching ends to
seal; continue coiling dough. Repeat procedure
with remaining dough to make an 8-inch flat circle.
Roll dough into a 13-inch circle; fit into a 9-inch
quiche dish or pieplate coated with cooking spray.
Fold edges under, and set aside.

Coat a nonstick skillet with cooking spray; add
oil, and place over medium heat until hot. Add
onion and garlic; sauté 8 minutes or until lightly
browned. Spread onion mixture in bottom of prepared crust; sprinkle with cheese. Arrange tomato
slices over cheese; top with basil.

Combine milk and next 4 ingredients in container of an electric blender; cover and process
until smooth. Pour over tomato. Bake at 350° for 45
minutes or until a knife inserted 1 inch from center
comes out clean; let stand 10 minutes. Yield: 6
servings.

PER SERVING: 207 CALORIES (30% FROM FAT)
FAT 6.9G (SATURATED FAT 2.8G)
PROTEIN 12.4G   CARBOHYDRATE 18.0G
CHOLESTEROL 84MG   SODIUM 341MG

ARTICHOKE-BASIL QUICHE

*The rice crust for this quiche offers a low-fat
alternative to a standard pastry crust.*

2 cups cooked brown rice (cooked without salt
   or fat)
1¼ cups (5 ounces) shredded part-skim
   mozzarella cheese, divided
1 egg white, lightly beaten
¼ teaspoon dried dillweed
Vegetable cooking spray
1 teaspoon margarine
½ cup chopped sweet red pepper
¼ cup sliced green onions
1 clove garlic, minced
½ cup shredded fresh basil
1 (14-ounce) can artichoke hearts, drained and
   sliced
1 cup evaporated skimmed milk
1 teaspoon dried thyme
2 eggs

Combine rice, ¼ cup mozzarella cheese, egg
white, and dillweed in a bowl, stirring well. Spread
rice mixture in bottom and up sides of a 9-inch
pieplate coated with cooking spray. Bake at 350°
for 5 minutes. Set aside.

Melt margarine in a small nonstick skillet over
medium-high heat. Add red pepper, green onions,
and garlic; sauté until vegetables are tender. Stir in
shredded basil; spread over prepared crust. Sprinkle with remaining 1 cup cheese. Arrange artichoke
slices over cheese.

Combine milk, thyme, and eggs in container of
an electric blender; cover and process until smooth.
Pour over vegetables.

Bake at 350° for 1 hour or until a knife inserted
in center comes out clean. Let stand 10 minutes
before serving. Yield: 6 servings.

PER SERVING: 224 CALORIES (29% FROM FAT)
FAT 7.1G (SATURATED FAT 3.3G)
PROTEIN 14.5G   CARBOHYDRATE 26.0G
CHOLESTEROL 89MG   SODIUM 324MG

ARTICHOKE-CHEDDAR STRATA

Vegetable cooking spray
1 teaspoon margarine
½ cup chopped green onions
3 slices whole wheat bread, cubed
¾ cup (3 ounces) shredded reduced-fat Cheddar cheese
1 (14-ounce) can artichoke hearts, drained and quartered
1 (4-ounce) jar sliced pimiento, drained
¾ cup frozen egg substitute, thawed
1 (12-ounce) can evaporated skimmed milk
½ teaspoon dry mustard
⅛ teaspoon ground red pepper

Coat a small nonstick skillet with cooking spray; add margarine. Place over medium heat until margarine melts. Add chopped green onions; sauté 3 to 4 minutes or until tender. Remove from heat, and set aside.

Arrange half of bread cubes in a 9-inch quiche dish coated with cooking spray. Top with half of cheese, half of artichokes, half of green onions, and half of pimiento. Repeat layers with remaining bread cubes, cheese, artichokes, green onions, and pimiento.

Combine egg substitute and next 3 ingredients; stir well. Pour over mixture in quiche dish. Cover and chill at least 3 hours or overnight.

Let stand at room temperature 30 minutes. Bake, uncovered, at 350° for 1 hour or until set. Yield: 6 servings.

PER SERVING: 179 CALORIES (22% FROM FAT)
FAT 4.3G (SATURATED FAT 1.9G)
PROTEIN 15.0G CARBOHYDRATE 21.4G
CHOLESTEROL 12MG SODIUM 445MG

BROCCOLI-CAULIFLOWER CHEESE STRATA

2 cups small fresh broccoli flowerets
1½ cups small fresh cauliflower flowerets
6 (1-ounce) slices French bread, cut into ½-inch cubes
Vegetable cooking spray
¾ cup (3 ounces) shredded reduced-fat sharp Cheddar cheese, divided
1 cup 1% low-fat milk
2 (8-ounce) cartons frozen egg substitute, thawed
¼ cup thinly sliced green onions
¼ teaspoon salt
⅛ teaspoon dry mustard
⅛ teaspoon ground red pepper
6 thin slices unpeeled tomato
1½ teaspoons grated Parmesan cheese
Black pepper (optional)

Arrange broccoli and cauliflower in a vegetable steamer, and place over boiling water. Cover and steam 5 minutes or until crisp-tender. Drain and plunge into cold water; drain again.

Arrange bread cubes evenly in the bottom of an 11- x 7- x 1½-inch baking dish coated with cooking spray. Top with ½ cup Cheddar cheese. Arrange broccoli and cauliflower on top of cheese.

Combine milk and next 5 ingredients in a bowl; stir well, and pour over vegetables. Cover with aluminum foil coated with cooking spray; chill 1 hour.

Cut 10 (1-inch) slits in foil. Bake at 350° for 1 hour and 15 minutes or until liquid is absorbed. Uncover and top with remaining ¼ cup Cheddar cheese. Arrange tomato slices in a single layer on top of strata, and top with Parmesan cheese. Sprinkle with black pepper, if desired. Bake at 350° for 8 minutes. Let stand 5 minutes before serving. Yield: 6 servings.

PER SERVING: 202 CALORIES (19% FROM FAT)
FAT 4.3G (SATURATED FAT 2.1G)
PROTEIN 17.3G CARBOHYDRATE 23.1G
CHOLESTEROL 12MG SODIUM 522MG

LIGHT VEGETABLE CHEESE STRATA

Vegetable cooking spray
1 teaspoon reduced-calorie margarine
2 tablespoons minced shallots
1 teaspoon minced garlic
1 cup sliced fresh mushrooms
1 cup diced zucchini
1 cup diced green pepper
2½ cups skim milk
2 eggs, beaten
4 egg whites, lightly beaten
¼ teaspoon freshly ground pepper
⅛ teaspoon salt
6 cups cubed French bread
½ cup (2 ounces) shredded reduced-fat
    Cheddar cheese
¼ cup grated Parmesan cheese

Coat a large nonstick skillet with cooking spray. Add margarine, and place over medium-high heat until margarine melts. Add shallots and garlic; sauté until tender. Add mushrooms; sauté 5 minutes or until tender. Add zucchini and green pepper; sauté 5 minutes or until crisp-tender. Remove from heat, and set aside.

Combine milk, eggs, egg whites, pepper, and salt in a large bowl. Stir in vegetable mixture, bread cubes, and cheeses. Pour mixture into a 13- x 9- x 2-inch baking dish coated with cooking spray. Bake, uncovered, at 325° for 50 to 60 minutes or until lightly browned. Let stand 5 minutes. Cut into rectangles, and serve immediately. Yield: 8 servings.

PER SERVING: 183 CALORIES (24% FROM FAT)
FAT 4.9G (SATURATED FAT 2.2G)
PROTEIN 12.5G CARBOHYDRATE 21.3G
CHOLESTEROL 65MG SODIUM 398MG

CHEESE BLINTZES

1 cup 1% low-fat cottage cheese
1 cup light ricotta cheese
⅓ cup sugar
⅓ cup light process cream cheese
½ teaspoon vanilla extract
2 cups sliced fresh strawberries
¼ cup sugar
16 Crêpes

Combine first 5 ingredients in a food processor bowl; process until smooth. Place mixture in a bowl; cover and chill. Combine strawberries and sugar; toss and set aside. Spoon 2 tablespoons cheese mixture in center of each crêpe; fold sides and ends over. Place, seam side down, on a platter. Serve strawberry mixture over crêpes. Yield: 8 servings.

CRÊPES
1 cup skim milk
1 cup all-purpose flour
2 eggs
2 egg whites
⅛ teaspoon salt
Vegetable cooking spray

Combine first 5 ingredients in container of an electric blender; cover and process until smooth, scraping sides of container occasionally. Pour batter into a bowl; cover and chill at least 30 minutes.

Coat an 8-inch crêpe pan or nonstick skillet with cooking spray, and place over medium-high heat until hot. Remove pan from heat, and spoon 2 tablespoons batter into pan; quickly tilt pan in all directions so batter covers pan with a thin film. Cook about 1 minute.

Lift edge of crêpe to test for doneness. Crêpe is ready to turn when it can be shaken loose from pan. Turn crêpe over, and cook 30 seconds.

Place crêpe on a towel, and allow to cool. Repeat procedure until all batter is used. Stack crêpes between single layers of wax paper to prevent sticking. Yield: 16 crêpes.

PER SERVING: 224 CALORIES (19% FROM FAT)
FAT 4.8G (SATURATED FAT 2.2G)
PROTEIN 13.0G CARBOHYDRATE 33.3G
CHOLESTEROL 67MG SODIUM 272MG

SOUFFLÉED SPINACH CRÊPES

¼ cup plus 1 tablespoon grated Parmesan
    cheese, divided
3 tablespoons fine, dry breadcrumbs
1 tablespoon margarine, melted
2 teaspoons margarine
½ cup minced onion
1½ tablespoons all-purpose flour
⅔ cup skim milk
¼ teaspoon salt
⅛ teaspoon ground white pepper
⅛ teaspoon ground nutmeg
½ (10-ounce) package frozen chopped
    spinach, thawed and drained
1 egg yolk
3 egg whites
⅛ teaspoon cream of tartar
12 Parmesan Crêpes
Vegetable cooking spray
Fresh parsley sprigs (optional)

Combine 3 tablespoons Parmesan cheese, bread-crumbs, and 1 tablespoon melted margarine; stir well, and set aside.

Melt 2 teaspoons margarine in a small saucepan over medium heat. Add minced onion, and sauté 2 minutes or until tender. Add flour, and cook 1 minute, stirring constantly with a wire whisk. Gradually add skim milk, stirring constantly. Cook 1 minute or until thickened, stirring constantly. Stir in remaining 2 tablespoons Parmesan cheese, salt, white pepper, and nutmeg.

Position knife blade in food processor bowl; add sauce and spinach, and process until smooth. Add egg yolk; process until smooth.

Beat egg whites and cream of tartar at high speed of an electric mixer until stiff peaks form. Gently stir one-fourth of egg white mixture into spinach mixture. Gently fold remaining egg white mixture into spinach mixture.

Spoon ¼ cup spinach mixture over half of each crêpe, spreading to edge; fold crêpe in half and then in quarters. Arrange filled crêpes in each of 2 (11- x 7- x 1½-inch) baking dishes coated with cooking spray. Spoon breadcrumb mixture evenly over crêpes. Bake, uncovered, at 375° for 20 minutes. Serve with sliced tomatoes, and garnish with parsley, if desired. Yield: 6 servings.

PARMESAN CRÊPES

1¼ cups all-purpose flour
¼ cup grated Parmesan cheese
1½ cups skim milk
1 tablespoon margarine, melted
1 egg
Vegetable cooking spray

Combine flour and cheese in a medium bowl. Combine milk, margarine, and egg, stirring well; add to flour mixture, stirring with a wire whisk until almost smooth. Cover batter, and chill 1 hour.

Coat an 8-inch crêpe pan or nonstick skillet with cooking spray, and place over medium-high heat until hot. Remove pan from heat, and pour a scant ¼ cup batter into pan; quickly tilt pan in all directions so batter covers pan with a thin film. Cook about 1 minute.

Carefully lift edge of crêpe with spatula to test for doneness. The crêpe is ready to turn when it can be shaken loose from pan and the underside is lightly browned. Turn crêpe over, and cook 30 seconds on other side.

Place crêpe on a towel, and allow to cool. Repeat procedure until all of the batter is used. Stack crêpes between single layers of wax paper or paper towels to prevent sticking. Yield: 12 crêpes.

PER SERVING: 264 CALORIES (34% FROM FAT)
FAT 10.1G (SATURATED FAT 3.3G)
PROTEIN 13.7G CARBOHYDRATE 29.2G
CHOLESTEROL 80MG SODIUM 437MG

Add milk, margarine, and egg to the flour and cheese. Stir until the batter is smooth. Chill 1 hour or overnight.

Pour about ¼ cup batter into a preheated pan, tilting pan so batter covers the pan with a thin film.

Lift edge of crêpe to check for doneness. The crêpe should be light brown and easy to shake loose from the pan.

Souffléed Spinach Crêpes

Stuffed French Toast

STUFFED FRENCH TOAST

4 (1-ounce) diagonally cut slices French bread
    (about 1 inch thick)
3 tablespoons finely chopped dried apricots,
    divided
½ cup nonfat ricotta cheese
2 tablespoons (½ ounce) shredded part-skim
    mozzarella cheese
1 teaspoon sugar
¼ teaspoon vanilla extract
¾ cup apricot nectar
½ cup sliced ripe banana (about 1 small)
½ cup skim milk
¼ cup frozen egg substitute, thawed
Vegetable cooking spray

Cut a slit through top of each slice of bread to
form a pocket. Set aside.

Combine 1 tablespoon dried apricots, ricotta
cheese, mozzarella cheese, sugar, and vanilla in a
bowl; stir well. Stuff 2 tablespoons cheese mixture
into pocket of each slice of bread; set aside.

Combine remaining 2 tablespoons apricots and
apricot nectar in a small saucepan; bring to a boil.
Reduce heat, and simmer, uncovered, 1 minute.
Remove from heat; stir in banana. Set aside, and
keep warm.

Combine milk and egg substitute in a large shallow dish; stir well. Place stuffed bread slices in
dish, turning to coat. Let stand until milk mixture
is absorbed.

Coat a large nonstick skillet with cooking spray,
and place over medium heat until hot. Gently add
bread to skillet, and cook 2 minutes. Carefully turn
bread over, and cook 2 minutes or until browned.
Serve with warm apricot sauce. Yield: 2 servings.

PER SERVING: 392 CALORIES (7% FROM FAT)
FAT 3.1G (SATURATED FAT 1.2G)
PROTEIN 21.2G CARBOHYDRATE 72.0G
CHOLESTEROL 13MG SODIUM 482MG

PUFFY PINEAPPLE PANCAKE

1 small ripe pineapple, peeled and cored
Vegetable cooking spray
1 tablespoon margarine, melted
½ cup plus 1 tablespoon all-purpose flour
2 tablespoons dark brown sugar
¾ teaspoon baking powder
½ teaspoon ground cinnamon
¼ teaspoon salt
¾ cup skim milk
½ teaspoon vanilla extract
2 eggs, separated
1 egg white

Cut pineapple crosswise into ¼-inch-thick slices;
set 5 slices aside. Reserve remaining pineapple for
another use.

Coat a 9-inch pieplate with cooking spray; coat
with margarine. Arrange pineapple slices in pieplate, overlapping. Bake at 425° for 20 minutes,
and set aside.

Combine flour and next 4 ingredients in a large
bowl; stir well. Combine milk, vanilla, and egg
yolks; add to dry ingredients, stirring until smooth.
Beat 3 egg whites at high speed of an electric mixer
until soft peaks form; gently fold into flour mixture.

Pour batter evenly over pineapple. Bake at 425°
for 15 minutes or until puffed and golden. Remove
from oven; cut into wedges. Serve immediately.
Yield: 4 servings.

PER SERVING: 189 CALORIES (29% FROM FAT)
FAT 6.0G (SATURATED FAT 1.4G)
PROTEIN 7.5G CARBOHYDRATE 26.5G
CHOLESTEROL 107MG SODIUM 307MG

Buttermilk Pancakes with Orange Syrup

BUTTERMILK PANCAKES WITH ORANGE SYRUP

1 cup all-purpose flour
2 tablespoons sugar
1 teaspoon baking powder
½ teaspoon baking soda
1 cup nonfat buttermilk
1 tablespoon vegetable oil
1 egg, lightly beaten
Orange Syrup

Combine first 4 ingredients in a large bowl; stir well. Combine buttermilk, oil, and egg; add to dry ingredients, stirring until smooth. For each pancake, spoon ¼ cup batter onto a hot nonstick griddle. Turn pancakes when tops are covered with bubbles and edges look cooked. To serve, place 3 pancakes on each individual plate; top each serving with ½ cup Orange Syrup. Yield: 3 servings.

ORANGE SYRUP
¾ cup sugar
1 cup unsweetened orange juice
¾ cup fresh orange sections

Combine sugar and orange juice in a large saucepan. Bring to a boil over medium heat; cook 20 minutes or until reduced to 1 cup, stirring occasionally. Remove from heat; stir in oranges. Serve warm or chilled. Yield: 1½ cups.

PER SERVING: 454 CALORIES (14% FROM FAT)
FAT 7.1G (SATURATED FAT 1.7G)
PROTEIN 10.3G CARBOHYDRATE 88.9G
CHOLESTEROL 76MG SODIUM 323MG

CHEESE-FILLED BANANA PANCAKES

1½ cups sliced banana, divided
⅓ cup all-purpose flour
⅓ cup nonfat buttermilk
1 tablespoon sugar
½ teaspoon vanilla extract
1 egg
⅓ cup light process cream cheese
2 tablespoons brown sugar
½ teaspoon vanilla extract
Vegetable cooking spray

Combine ½ cup banana, flour, and next 4 ingredients in container of an electric blender; cover and process until smooth, scraping sides of container. Pour batter into a bowl; cover and chill 15 minutes.

Beat cream cheese, brown sugar, and vanilla at medium speed of an electric mixer until light and fluffy; set aside.

Spoon about ¼ cup batter onto a hot nonstick griddle or nonstick skillet coated with cooking spray. Turn pancake when top is covered with bubbles and edges look cooked. Repeat with remaining batter to make 8 pancakes.

Place 1 pancake on each of two serving plates. Spread 1 tablespoon cheese mixture over each pancake; arrange 2 tablespoons sliced banana over each serving. Repeat procedure with remaining pancakes, cheese mixture, and banana, ending with banana. Yield: 2 servings.

PER SERVING: 394 CALORIES (23% FROM FAT)
FAT 9.9G (SATURATED FAT 4.9G)
PROTEIN 11.6G   CARBOHYDRATE 66.2G
CHOLESTEROL 129MG   SODIUM 294MG

ZUCCHINI WAFFLES WITH PIMENTO-CHEESE SAUCE

2 teaspoons margarine
1 tablespoon plus 2 teaspoons all-purpose flour
⅛ teaspoon salt
⅛ teaspoon dry mustard
Dash of ground pepper
1 cup 2% low-fat milk
½ cup (2 ounces) shredded reduced-fat sharp
   Cheddar cheese
1 (2-ounce) jar diced pimento, drained
1¼ cups all-purpose flour
1½ teaspoons baking powder
¼ teaspoon dried basil
¼ teaspoon baking soda
¼ teaspoon salt
⅛ teaspoon coarsely ground pepper
1 cup nonfat buttermilk
1 cup shredded zucchini
½ cup no-salt-added cream-style corn
⅓ cup sliced green onions
2 teaspoons vegetable oil
1 egg, lightly beaten
Vegetable cooking spray

Melt margarine in a saucepan over medium heat. Add 1 tablespoon plus 2 teaspoons flour and next 3 ingredients; cook 1 minute, stirring constantly. Add milk, stirring with a wire whisk until blended. Cook 5 minutes or until thickened and bubbly, stirring constantly. Remove from heat; add cheese and pimento, stirring until cheese melts. Keep warm.

Combine 1¼ cups flour and next 5 ingredients; stir well. Combine buttermilk and next 5 ingredients; add to dry ingredients, stirring just until moistened.

Coat a waffle iron with cooking spray, and preheat. Spoon about ⅓ cup of batter per 4-inch waffle onto hot waffle iron, spreading batter to edges. Cook 5 minutes or until steaming stops; repeat procedure with remaining batter. For each serving, spoon ¼ cup sauce over 2 waffles. Yield: 4 servings.

PER SERVING: 329 CALORIES (28% FROM FAT)
FAT 10.3G (SATURATED FAT 3.7G)
PROTEIN 15.3G   CARBOHYDRATE 45.0G
CHOLESTEROL 70MG   SODIUM 511MG

Gingerbread Waffles with Maple Topping

GINGERBREAD WAFFLES WITH MAPLE TOPPING

2 tablespoons reduced-calorie stick margarine, softened
2 tablespoons molasses
1 egg
1 cup all-purpose flour
⅓ cup whole wheat flour
1 teaspoon baking powder
½ teaspoon baking soda
1 teaspoon ground ginger
¼ teaspoon ground cinnamon
⅛ teaspoon ground cloves
¾ cup skim milk
1 egg white
Vegetable cooking spray
Maple Topping

Beat margarine and molasses at medium-high speed of an electric mixer until smooth; add egg, beating well.

Combine all-purpose flour and next 6 ingredients, stirring well. Add flour mixture to creamed mixture alternately with milk, beginning and ending with flour mixture. Beat just until blended after each addition.

Beat egg white at high speed of an electric mixer until stiff peaks form. Gently fold into batter.

Coat an 8-inch-square waffle iron with cooking spray; allow waffle iron to preheat. Pour 2 cups batter onto hot waffle iron, spreading batter to edges. Bake 4 to 5 minutes or until steaming stops. Repeat procedure with remaining batter.

To serve, place 2 (4-inch) waffles on each individual serving plate. Top each serving with 2 tablespoons Maple Topping. Yield: 4 servings.

MAPLE TOPPING
¼ cup light ricotta cheese
1½ tablespoons honey
¼ cup vanilla low-fat yogurt
¼ teaspoon maple flavoring

Combine cheese and honey in container of an electric blender or food processor; cover and process until smooth. Transfer mixture to a small bowl. Add yogurt and flavoring; stir well. Cover and chill until ready to use. Yield: ½ cup.

PER SERVING: 296 CALORIES (20% FROM FAT)
FAT 6.6G (SATURATED FAT 1.0G)
PROTEIN 11.0G   CARBOHYDRATE 50.2G
CHOLESTEROL 60MG   SODIUM 292MG

OPEN-FACED BREAKFAST SANDWICHES

Vegetable cooking spray
½ cup sliced fresh mushrooms
2 tablespoons chopped green pepper
1½ cups frozen egg substitute, thawed
2 tablespoons skim milk
¼ teaspoon onion powder
⅛ teaspoon salt
8 tomato slices (½ inch thick)
4 (2-ounce) English muffins, split and toasted
1 cup (4 ounces) shredded reduced-fat sharp Cheddar cheese
⅛ teaspoon pepper

Coat a medium nonstick skillet with cooking spray; place over medium-high heat until hot. Add mushrooms and green pepper; sauté until tender.

Combine egg substitute and next 3 ingredients; stir well. Pour over mixture in skillet; cook over medium heat, stirring frequently, until egg substitute is firm but still moist. Remove from heat.

Place a tomato slice on each muffin half; top each with 2 tablespoons egg mixture and 2 tablespoons cheese. Sprinkle with pepper.

Place muffin halves on a baking sheet. Broil 5½ inches from heat (with electric oven door partially opened) 1 minute or until cheese melts. Yield: 8 servings.

PER SERVING: 166 CALORIES (20% FROM FAT)
FAT 3.6G (SATURATED FAT 1.8G)
PROTEIN 11.9G   CARBOHYDRATE 21.3G
CHOLESTEROL 10MG   SODIUM 379MG

GRITS CASSEROLE

5 cups water
1¼ cups regular grits, uncooked
½ cup chopped onion
2 small cloves garlic, crushed
¼ teaspoon salt
¼ teaspoon pepper
½ cup skim milk
½ cup frozen egg substitute, thawed
½ cup (2 ounces) shredded sharp Cheddar
   cheese
Vegetable cooking spray

Bring water to a boil; gradually stir in grits and next 4 ingredients. Reduce heat, and simmer, uncovered, 25 minutes or until thickened, stirring occasionally. Remove from heat. Combine milk and egg substitute in a bowl. Gradually stir into hot grits mixture with a wire whisk. Add cheese; stir well.

Spoon into an 8-inch square baking dish coated with cooking spray. Bake, uncovered, at 375° for 45 minutes or until set. Yield: 6 (1-cup) servings.

PER SERVING: 176 CALORIES (18% FROM FAT)
FAT 3.5G (SATURATED FAT 2.0G)
PROTEIN 8.1G CARBOHYDRATE 28.0G
CHOLESTEROL 10MG SODIUM 199MG

MAMA'S POLENTA

2 (10-ounce) packages frozen chopped
   spinach, thawed and drained
2 tablespoons all-purpose flour
1 cup evaporated skimmed milk
¼ cup canned vegetable or chicken broth,
   undiluted
¼ cup water
2 teaspoons dry sherry
¼ teaspoon salt
¼ teaspoon black pepper
⅛ teaspoon ground red pepper
½ cup grated Parmesan cheese, divided
Basic Polenta
Vegetable cooking spray
4 hard-cooked eggs, peeled and sliced

Press spinach between paper towels until barely moist, and set aside.

Combine flour and milk in a small saucepan, stirring with a wire whisk until blended; cook 1 minute, stirring constantly. Gradually add vegetable broth and next 5 ingredients, stirring with a wire whisk. Cook over medium heat 10 minutes or until thickened and bubbly, stirring constantly. Remove from heat, and stir in ¼ cup Parmesan cheese. Set aside.

Prepare Basic Polenta, and spread in bottom of a 13- x 9- x 2-inch baking dish coated with cooking spray. Spread spinach evenly over polenta. Arrange egg slices evenly over spinach. Pour cheese sauce over egg slices, and sprinkle with remaining ¼ cup Parmesan cheese. Bake at 350° for 30 minutes or until lightly browned. Let stand 15 minutes before serving. Yield: 8 servings.

BASIC POLENTA
1¼ cups cornmeal
½ teaspoon salt
4 cups water

Place cornmeal and salt in a large saucepan. Gradually add water, stirring constantly with a wire whisk. Bring to a boil; reduce heat to medium. Cook, uncovered, 15 minutes, stirring frequently. Yield: 4 (1-cup) servings.

PER SERVING: 191 CALORIES (23% FROM FAT)
FAT 4.9G (SATURATED FAT 1.9G)
PROTEIN 11.8G CARBOHYDRATE 25.3G
CHOLESTEROL 111MG SODIUM 466MG

Did You Know?

Polenta, a staple of northern Italy, is made simply from cornmeal, water, and salt. It tastes creamy, rich, and wholesome, and is loaded with carbohydrates. Here, polenta is suggested as part of a brunch dish, but it is often served with dinner.

Gradually add water to corn-meal and salt, stirring with a wire whisk.

Bring cornmeal mixture to a boil, and reduce heat to medium.

Cook polenta 15 minutes, stir-ring frequently. (Mixture will bubble and spatter.)

Mama's Polenta

Chunky Minestrone (recipe on page 54)

SOUPS & SANDWICHES

A bowl of hearty soup or stew is quite a comfort after a long day. And some of the best are loaded with healthy, vitamin-rich vegetables. Chunky Minestrone and Quick Bean Soup (both on page 54) are two of the favorites in this chapter.

Vegetarian soups can be even more satisfying when paired with a meatless sandwich. For starters, combine Corn and Pepper Chowder (page 58) with Welsh Rarebit (page 61). Or serve Curried Lentil Soup (page 54) with one of the pita sandwiches on pages 68 and 69. Whatever your choice, enjoy!

Light Beer-Cheese Soup

LIGHT BEER-CHEESE SOUP

3½ cups skim milk, divided
¼ cup cornstarch
⅔ cup water
⅔ cup canned vegetable or chicken broth, undiluted
1 tablespoon white wine Worcestershire sauce
¼ to ½ teaspoon ground red pepper
¼ teaspoon garlic powder
1½ cups (6 ounces) finely shredded reduced-fat Cheddar cheese
½ cup flat light beer
⅓ cup nonfat sour cream
Toast Triangles
1 tablespoon finely shredded reduced-fat Cheddar cheese
Paprika (optional)

Combine ½ cup milk and cornstarch; stir well. Set cornstarch mixture aside.

Combine remaining 3 cups milk, water, and next 4 ingredients in a large saucepan. Cook over medium heat until thoroughly heated. Add cornstarch mixture, stirring well. Cook over low heat, stirring constantly, until thickened and bubbly.

Add 1½ cups cheese; cook, stirring constantly, until cheese melts and mixture is smooth. Stir in beer and sour cream. Cook just until thoroughly heated, stirring occasionally. Ladle soup into individual bowls. Top each serving with 3 Toast Triangles, and sprinkle with ½ teaspoon cheese and paprika, if desired. Yield: 6 (1-cup) servings.

TOAST TRIANGLES

3 (¾-ounce) slices reduced-calorie white bread
Butter-flavored vegetable cooking spray

Trim crust from bread slices. Cut each slice into 4 squares; cut each square into 2 triangles. Place 18 triangles on an ungreased baking sheet; reserve remaining triangles for another use. Spray both sides of each triangle with cooking spray. Bake at 350° for 10 to 12 minutes or until triangles are dry and lightly browned. Yield: 18 triangles.

PER SERVING: 202 CALORIES (29% FROM FAT)
FAT 6.7G (SATURATED FAT 3.5G)
PROTEIN 15.2G CARBOHYDRATE 19.6G
CHOLESTEROL 23MG SODIUM 482MG

BLACK BEAN SOUP

3 cups dried black beans
10 cups water
1 teaspoon salt
1 cup chopped celery
1 cup chopped onion
1 cup chopped green pepper
1 cup sliced carrot
2 teaspoons dried basil
2 teaspoons dried oregano
1 teaspoon black pepper
½ teaspoon ground cumin
¼ to ½ teaspoon ground red pepper
4 cloves garlic, minced
1 bay leaf
2 (14½-ounce) cans no-salt-added whole tomatoes, undrained and chopped
1 (11-ounce) can vacuum-packed white corn
1 (8-ounce) can no-salt-added tomato sauce

Sort and wash beans; place in a large Dutch oven or stockpot. Add 10 cups water and salt, and bring to a boil; cook 1 minute. Remove from heat; cover and let stand 1 hour. (Do not drain beans.)

Add celery and next 10 ingredients to beans. Bring mixture to a boil; cover, reduce heat, and simmer 1½ hours or until beans are tender.

Add tomatoes, corn, and tomato sauce; stir well. Bring to a boil; reduce heat, and simmer, uncovered, 30 minutes. Discard bay leaf. Yield: 12 (1½-cup) servings.

PER SERVING: 227 CALORIES (4% FROM FAT)
FAT 1.0G (SATURATED FAT 0.2G)
PROTEIN 12.7G CARBOHYDRATE 45.4G
CHOLESTEROL 0MG SODIUM 295MG

QUICK BEAN SOUP

6 cups tightly packed chopped fresh kale
   (about ¾ pound)
1 cup chopped onion
3 (16-ounce) cans red kidney beans, undrained
2 (14½-ounce) cans no-salt-added whole
   tomatoes, undrained and chopped
1 (15-ounce) can garbanzo beans, undrained
1 cup water
⅔ cup canned vegetable or chicken broth,
   undiluted
1 teaspoon garlic powder
1 teaspoon onion powder

Combine all ingredients in a large Dutch oven; bring to a boil. Cover, reduce heat, and simmer 1 hour. Yield: 13 (1-cup) servings.

PER SERVING: 207 CALORIES (5% FROM FAT)
FAT 1.1G (SATURATED FAT 0.2G)
PROTEIN 12.6G CARBOHYDRATE 38.8G
CHOLESTEROL 0MG SODIUM 480MG

CHUNKY MINESTRONE

(pictured on page 50)

2 teaspoons olive oil
1½ cups chopped onion
1 medium carrot, halved lengthwise and sliced
   (about ¾ cup)
1 clove garlic, minced
½ cup long-grain rice, uncooked
2½ cups water
1¼ cups canned vegetable or chicken broth,
   undiluted
2 (14½-ounce) cans no-salt-added whole
   tomatoes, undrained and chopped
1 teaspoon dried Italian seasoning
1 medium zucchini, halved lengthwise and
   sliced (about 2 cups)
1 (15-ounce) can cannellini beans, drained
1 (10-ounce) package frozen chopped spinach,
   thawed and drained
¼ teaspoon pepper
⅔ cup grated Parmesan cheese

Heat oil in a large Dutch oven over medium-high heat. Add onion, carrot, and garlic; sauté 3 minutes. Add rice and next 4 ingredients; bring to a boil. Cover, reduce heat, and simmer 20 minutes. Add zucchini and next 3 ingredients; cook an additional 5 minutes. Ladle into individual soup bowls, and sprinkle with cheese. Yield: 7 (1½-cup) servings.

PER SERVING: 187 CALORIES (21% FROM FAT)
FAT 4.3G (SATURATED FAT 1.7G)
PROTEIN 9.0G CARBOHYDRATE 29.1G
CHOLESTEROL 6MG SODIUM 375MG

CURRIED LENTIL SOUP

Vegetable cooking spray
2 teaspoons vegetable oil
2 cups chopped onion (about 2 medium)
6 cloves garlic, minced
¾ cup dried lentils, uncooked
1 (19-ounce) can garbanzo beans, drained
3¾ cups water
1 (14½-ounce) can vegetable or chicken broth
1 tablespoon peeled, grated gingerroot
1 teaspoon ground cumin
1 teaspoon ground coriander
½ teaspoon dried crushed red pepper
½ teaspoon curry powder
1 cup seeded, chopped fresh tomato
¼ teaspoon salt
½ cup nonfat sour cream

Coat a Dutch oven with cooking spray; add oil, and place over medium-high heat until hot. Add onion and garlic; sauté 5 minutes or until tender.
Add lentils and next 8 ingredients; stir well. Bring to a boil; cover, reduce heat, and simmer 25 to 35 minutes or until lentils are tender.
Stir in tomato and salt. Ladle soup into individual bowls. Top each serving with 1 tablespoon sour cream. Yield: 8 (1-cup) servings.

PER SERVING: 181 CALORIES (14% FROM FAT)
FAT 2.9G (SATURATED FAT 0.4G)
PROTEIN 10.7G CARBOHYDRATE 29.3G
CHOLESTEROL 0MG SODIUM 404MG

Curried Lentil Soup

Lentil Soup with Gruyère Gremolada

2 cardamom pods
1 teaspoon cumin seeds
¼ teaspoon dried crushed red pepper
1 tablespoon vegetable oil
1½ cups finely chopped onion
4 cloves garlic, minced
3 cups chopped unpeeled tomato
1 cup dried lentils, uncooked
¾ teaspoon salt
6 cups water
2 cups chopped fresh kale
¾ cup (3 ounces) grated Gruyère cheese
1 tablespoon plus 1 teaspoon grated lemon rind
1 tablespoon chopped fresh thyme
2 cloves garlic, minced

Remove outer shell of cardamom pods, reserving seeds; discard shells.

Combine cardamom seeds, cumin, and red pepper in a Dutch oven; cook over medium-low heat 10 minutes, stirring occasionally. Crush seed mixture, using a mortar and pestle; set aside.

Heat oil in pan over medium heat. Add onion and 4 cloves garlic; sauté 5 minutes or until tender. Add crushed seed mixture, tomato, and next 3 ingredients; bring to a boil. Cover, reduce heat, and simmer 20 minutes. Uncover and simmer 10 minutes or until lentils are tender.

Place 2 cups lentil mixture in container of an electric blender; cover and process until smooth. Return lentil puree to pan; stir in kale. Bring to a simmer, and cook, uncovered, 5 minutes or until kale is tender.

To make gremolada, combine cheese, lemon rind, thyme, and 2 cloves minced garlic. Stir well.

Ladle soup into individual soup bowls; top with gremolada. Yield: 6 (1½-cup) servings.

Note: Whole spices can be crushed in a heavy-duty, zip-top plastic bag, using a meat mallet or a rolling pin instead of using a mortar and pestle.

PER SERVING: 241 CALORIES (29% FROM FAT)
FAT 7.8G (SATURATED FAT 3.2G)
PROTEIN 15.5G   CARBOHYDRATE 30.2G
CHOLESTEROL 16MG   SODIUM 364MG

Sherried Mushroom and Rice Soup

Vegetable cooking spray
1½ teaspoons reduced-calorie margarine
¾ cup finely chopped celery
¼ cup chopped onion
2 ounces fresh shiitake mushrooms, chopped
2 teaspoons all-purpose flour
1¼ cups evaporated skimmed milk, divided
2 tablespoons dry sherry
⅛ teaspoon pepper
Dash of salt
½ cup cooked long-grain rice (cooked without salt or fat)

Coat a large nonstick skillet with cooking spray; add margarine. Place over medium-high heat until margarine melts. Add celery, onion, and mushrooms; sauté 3 to 4 minutes or until tender.

Combine flour and 2 tablespoons milk, stirring until smooth; add to vegetable mixture. Add remaining 1 cup plus 2 tablespoons milk, sherry, pepper, and salt; cook, stirring constantly, until mixture is thickened. Stir in rice; reduce heat to low, and simmer 10 minutes. Yield: 2 servings.

PER SERVING: 233 CALORIES (11% FROM FAT)
FAT 2.8G (SATURATED FAT 0.2G)
PROTEIN 14.6G   CARBOHYDRATE 38.0G
CHOLESTEROL 6MG   SODIUM 337MG

Many of the soup recipes call for canned vegetable broth. Our nutritional analyses are based on regular broth, which does contain sodium. If you're watching your sodium intake, look for no-salt-added vegetable broth at the supermarket.

Or you can make your own no-salt-added vegetable broth. Just cook a variety of vegetables, including onion, celery, and carrots, in a stockpot with water. Simmer 1 hour, and then strain.

WISCONSIN CHEESE CHOWDER

Vegetable cooking spray
3 cups diced carrot
1 cup sliced celery
¾ cup chopped green onions
4 cups peeled, diced round red potato (about
    1½ pounds)
⅔ cup water
⅔ cup canned vegetable or chicken broth,
    diluted
⅓ cup all-purpose flour
2 cups 2% low-fat milk
¼ teaspoon ground white pepper
¼ teaspoon ground nutmeg
¾ cup dry white wine
¾ cup (3 ounces) shredded sharp Cheddar
    cheese
¼ cup (1 ounce) shredded Swiss cheese

Coat a large Dutch oven with cooking spray; place over medium-high heat until hot. Add carrot, celery, and green onions; sauté 8 minutes. Add potato, water, and vegetable broth; bring to a boil. Cover, reduce heat, and simmer 25 minutes or until tender.

Place flour in a medium bowl. Gradually add milk, blending with a wire whisk; add to pan. Stir in pepper and nutmeg; cook 2 minutes or until thickened. Add wine; cook 1 minute. Remove from heat; add cheeses, stirring until cheeses melt. Yield: 6 (1½-cup) servings.

PER SERVING: 267 CALORIES (27% FROM FAT)
FAT 8.0G (SATURATED FAT 4.9G)
PROTEIN 11.6G   CARBOHYDRATE 38.0G
CHOLESTEROL 26MG   SODIUM 302MG

Wisconsin Cheese Chowder

CORN AND PEPPER CHOWDER

Serve this soup with Welsh Rarebit (page 61) or a simple grilled cheese for a hearty lunch or light supper.

Vegetable cooking spray
1 teaspoon olive oil
1 cup chopped onion
1 cup diced sweet red pepper
2½ tablespoons all-purpose flour
½ teaspoon ground cumin
⅛ teaspoon ground red pepper
1 cup water
1 cup canned vegetable or chicken broth
1¼ cups peeled, diced potato
2 cups frozen whole kernel corn
1 cup evaporated skimmed milk
2 tablespoons canned chopped green chiles, drained
¼ teaspoon pepper

Coat a large Dutch oven with cooking spray; add oil. Place over medium-high heat until hot. Add onion and sweet red pepper; sauté 5 minutes or until vegetables are tender.

Stir flour, cumin, and ground red pepper into sautéed vegetables; cook 1 minute, stirring constantly. Gradually stir in water; add vegetable broth and potato. Bring mixture to a boil, stirring frequently. Cover, reduce heat, and simmer 10 minutes or until potato is tender and mixture is thickened.

Add corn and remaining ingredients; cook until thoroughly heated, stirring occasionally. Yield: 6 (1-cup) servings.

PER SERVING: 151 CALORIES (11% FROM FAT)
FAT 1.8G (SATURATED FAT 0.3G)
PROTEIN 6.5G CARBOHYDRATE 28.8G
CHOLESTEROL 2MG SODIUM 224MG

CHILI WITH GIANT POLENTA CROUTONS

Vegetable cooking spray
3 cups water
1¼ cups yellow cornmeal
¼ teaspoon salt
1 teaspoon vegetable oil
3 cups coarsely chopped onion
3 cloves garlic, minced
2 (16-ounce) cans red kidney beans, undrained
2 (14½-ounce) cans no-salt-added whole tomatoes, undrained and chopped
1½ tablespoons chili powder
2 tablespoons no-salt-added tomato paste
2 teaspoons ground cumin
½ cup (2 ounces) finely shredded sharp Cheddar cheese

Coat a 9-inch square baking pan with cooking spray; set aside.

Bring water to a boil in a large saucepan. Slowly add cornmeal and salt, stirring constantly with a wire whisk until smooth. Spoon into prepared pan, and spread evenly; set aside.

Add oil to saucepan; place over medium heat until hot. Add onion and garlic; sauté 5 minutes or until tender. Add beans and next 4 ingredients; stir well. Reduce heat, and cook, uncovered, 15 minutes, stirring frequently.

Cut cornmeal mixture (polenta) into 16 (2¼-inch) squares. Coat a large nonstick skillet with cooking spray, and place over medium heat until hot. Add cornmeal pieces, and cook 3 minutes on each side or until lightly browned.

Ladle 1 cup chili into each of 8 soup bowls. Top each serving with 2 cornmeal squares and 1 tablespoon sharp Cheddar cheese. Yield: 8 servings.

PER SERVING: 260 CALORIES (15% FROM FAT)
FAT 4.2G (SATURATED FAT 1.8G)
PROTEIN 11.5G CARBOHYDRATE 45.9G
CHOLESTEROL 7MG SODIUM 543MG

Chili with Giant Polenta Croutons

Mozzarella Sandwich with Marinara Sauce

MOZZARELLA SANDWICHES WITH MARINARA SAUCE

Vegetable cooking spray
¼ cup chopped onion
1 clove garlic, minced
2 teaspoons minced fresh parsley
¼ teaspoon dried oregano
¼ teaspoon dried thyme
⅛ teaspoon salt
Dash of freshly ground pepper
½ (14½-ounce) can no-salt-added whole
    tomatoes, undrained and chopped
¼ cup dry red wine
¼ cup water
1½ tablespoons no-salt-added tomato paste
1 bay leaf
½ cup frozen egg substitute, thawed
½ cup skim milk
8 (1-ounce) slices part-skim mozzarella cheese
16 (½-ounce) slices French bread
¾ cup finely crushed shredded whole wheat
    cereal biscuits

Coat a small saucepan with cooking spray; place over medium-high heat until hot. Add onion and garlic; sauté until tender. Add parsley and next 4 ingredients; cook 30 seconds, stirring constantly. Add tomato, wine, water, tomato paste, and bay leaf, stirring to combine. Reduce heat, and simmer, uncovered, 20 to 30 minutes or until slightly thickened, stirring frequently. Remove and discard bay leaf. Set aside.

Combine egg substitute and milk in a shallow bowl, beating well. Set aside.

Place 1 cheese slice on each of 8 bread slices; top with remaining 8 bread slices.

Carefully dip sandwiches into egg substitute mixture, allowing excess to drip off. Sprinkle each sandwich with crushed cereal. Place sandwiches on a large baking sheet coated with cooking spray. Bake at 400° for 3 minutes; turn sandwiches, and bake an additional 4 to 6 minutes or until crisp and golden. Serve immediately with warm marinara sauce. Yield: 8 servings.

PER SERVING: 213 CALORIES (23% FROM FAT)
FAT 5.5G (SATURATED FAT 3.1G)
PROTEIN 12.9G CARBOHYDRATE 27.5G
CHOLESTEROL 18MG SODIUM 370MG

WELSH RAREBIT

¾ cup evaporated skimmed milk
1 cup (4 ounces) shredded reduced-fat sharp
    Cheddar cheese
1 teaspoon Dijon mustard
½ teaspoon low-sodium Worcestershire sauce
⅛ teaspoon lemon juice
Dash of ground red pepper
8 (¾-inch-thick) slices French bread, toasted

Pour milk into a small saucepan; place over medium heat. Cook, stirring constantly, until milk is thoroughly heated (do not boil). Add cheese and next 4 ingredients, stirring until cheese melts and mixture is smooth. Reduce heat to low, and cook 2 minutes, stirring frequently.

To serve, place bread on individual serving plates, and top each slice with 2 tablespoons cheese sauce. Serve immediately. Yield: 8 servings.

PER SERVING: 159 CALORIES (22% FROM FAT)
FAT 3.8G (SATURATED FAT 1.8G)
PROTEIN 9.0G CARBOHYDRATE 21.7G
CHOLESTEROL 12MG SODIUM 341MG

GRILLED BLUE CHEESE SANDWICHES

1 cup 1% low-fat cottage cheese
¼ cup torn fresh watercress
¼ cup crumbled blue cheese
2 tablespoons finely chopped walnuts
1 tablespoon nonfat mayonnaise
1 teaspoon low-sodium Worcestershire sauce
2 drops of hot sauce
10 (¾-ounce) slices reduced-calorie whole
    wheat bread
5 tomato slices (¼ inch thick)
Butter-flavored vegetable cooking spray

Place cottage cheese in container of an electric blender or food processor; cover and process on high speed 30 seconds or until smooth, stopping once to scrape down sides. Transfer to a small bowl. Stir in watercress and next 5 ingredients. Spread cheese mixture evenly over 5 slices of bread, and place tomato slices over cheese mixture. Top with remaining 5 bread slices.

Transfer sandwiches to a sandwich press or hot griddle coated with cooking spray. Cook until bread is lightly browned and cheese melts. Yield: 5 servings.

PER SERVING: 160 CALORIES (23% FROM FAT)
FAT 4.0G (SATURATED FAT 1.5G)
PROTEIN 11.8G CARBOHYDRATE 21.8G
CHOLESTEROL 6MG SODIUM 538MG

FYI

A skillet of melted butter is not a prerequisite for golden, crispy, grilled sandwiches. To grill sandwiches without adding fat, coat a nonstick skillet with cooking spray, and allow the skillet to get hot.

Add sandwiches, and press them down with a spatula or set a heavy lid (slightly smaller than the skillet) directly on them. The weight of the lid presses against the sandwiches, ensuring crisp bread. The lid also holds in heat that melts the cheese and warms the sandwiches throughout.

WARM ASPARAGUS SANDWICHES

1 cup 1% low-fat cottage cheese
1 tablespoon plus 2 teaspoons freshly grated
    Parmesan cheese, divided
1 teaspoon chopped green onions
2 teaspoons lemon juice
16 fresh asparagus spears (about 10 ounces)
8 (1-ounce) slices white bread
8 (1-ounce) slices whole wheat bread
Vegetable cooking spray
1 tablespoon plus 1 teaspoon reduced-calorie
    margarine, melted

Position knife blade in food processor bowl; add
cottage cheese, 2 teaspoons Parmesan cheese,
green onions, and lemon juice. Process until smooth;
set aside.

Snap off tough ends of asparagus. Remove scales
from stalks with a knife or vegetable peeler, if
desired. Arrange asparagus in a vegetable steamer
over boiling water. Cover and steam 4 to 5 minutes
or until crisp-tender.

Trim crust from bread slices; reserve for another
use. Roll each slice to 1/8-inch thickness with a
rolling pin. Spread 1 tablespoon cottage cheese
mixture over each slice. Place an asparagus spear
on each slice, and roll up. Place seam side down on
a baking sheet coated with cooking spray. Brush
with melted margarine, and sprinkle with remaining 1 tablespoon Parmesan cheese. Bake at 400° for
10 minutes or until golden. Yield: 8 servings.

PER SERVING: 189 CALORIES (18% FROM FAT)
FAT 3.7G (SATURATED FAT 0.9G)
PROTEIN 10.1G CARBOHYDRATE 30.4G
CHOLESTEROL 4MG SODIUM 444MG

CAPRI SANDWICH

*You may use any ripe black olives instead of the
traditional Greek purple-black kalamata olives.*

2 teaspoons white wine vinegar
8 (1/4-inch-thick) slices unpeeled tomato (about
    2 medium)
1 (1-pound) loaf French bread
1 clove garlic, halved
1 (1-pound) unpeeled eggplant, cut crosswise
    into 1/2-inch slices
4 (1/4-inch-thick) slices onion
Vegetable cooking spray
2 tablespoons chopped fresh basil
1 tablespoon chopped kalamata olives
2 (1-ounce) slices provolone cheese, halved

Drizzle vinegar over tomato slices, and set aside.

Slice bread in half lengthwise; place, cut side up,
on a baking sheet. Broil 3 inches from heat (with
electric oven door partially opened) 30 seconds or
until lightly browned. Rub garlic on cut sides of
bread halves; discard garlic.

Arrange eggplant and onion slices in a single
layer on a baking sheet coated with cooking spray;
lightly coat eggplant and onion with cooking spray.
Broil 3 inches from heat 5 minutes; turn slices over,
and broil an additional 5 minutes or until lightly
browned.

Arrange eggplant and tomato on bottom half of
bread. Top with basil and olives, and set aside.
Arrange onion slices and provolone cheese on cut
side of top half of bread, and broil 3 inches from
heat for 30 seconds or until cheese melts. Place on
top of bottom half. To serve, cut loaf into 5 equal
pieces. Yield: 5 servings.

PER SERVING: 340 CALORIES (15% FROM FAT)
FAT 5.6G (SATURATED FAT 2.6G)
PROTEIN 12.5G CARBOHYDRATE 58.4G
CHOLESTEROL 11MG SODIUM 647MG

Capri Sandwich

RATATOUILLE-STUFFED LOAF

Vegetable cooking spray
1 tablespoon olive oil
½ cup chopped onion
1 clove garlic, minced
3 cups unpeeled, cubed eggplant
1 cup thinly sliced zucchini
½ cup chopped green pepper
1 medium unpeeled tomato, chopped
1 tablespoon chopped fresh parsley
¼ teaspoon dried oregano
¼ teaspoon dried basil
⅛ teaspoon pepper
1 cup (4 ounces) shredded part-skim mozzarella cheese
1 teaspoon lemon juice
1 (16-ounce) loaf Italian or French bread, about 15 inches long

Coat a large skillet with cooking spray; add oil, and place over medium heat until hot. Add onion and garlic, and sauté until tender. Add eggplant and zucchini; cover and cook 4 to 5 minutes. Add pepper and next 5 ingredients. Reduce heat, and simmer, uncovered, 6 to 8 minutes or until vegetables are tender; stir occasionally. Remove from heat; stir in cheese and lemon juice, and set aside.

Cut a ½-inch slice from each end of bread, using a long, serrated knife; set slices aside. Using a gentle sawing motion, hollow out center of loaf from each end, leaving a ½-inch shell resembling a tunnel. Reserve hollowed out portion of bread for another use. Secure 1 slice of bread to end of loaf with wooden picks. Stuff vegetable mixture into loaf; secure remaining slice of bread to end of loaf with wooden picks.

Place loaf on a baking sheet, and bake at 350° for 12 minutes or until thoroughly heated. Remove and discard end slices. Cut loaf into 6 equal slices, and serve warm. Yield: 6 servings.

PER SERVING: 240 CALORIES (23% FROM FAT)
FAT 6.0G (SATURATED FAT 2.4G)
PROTEIN 10.5G CARBOHYDRATE 36.2G
CHOLESTEROL 11MG SODIUM 398MG

ROASTED VEGETABLE PITAS

1 (1-pound) eggplant
1 tablespoon chopped fresh parsley
2 tablespoons fresh lemon juice
1 teaspoon olive oil
¼ teaspoon salt
⅛ teaspoon pepper
1 large clove garlic, crushed
1 medium-size sweet red pepper (about 7 ounces)
½ cup drained canned cannellini beans
½ teaspoon ground cumin
2 (6-inch) onion or plain pita bread rounds
¼ cup plain low-fat yogurt
2 tablespoons chopped green onions
Coarsely ground pepper

Pierce eggplant with a fork, and place on a baking sheet. Broil 5½ inches from heat (with electric oven door partially opened) 30 minutes or until very tender, turning frequently. Let cool; peel and coarsely chop. Combine eggplant, parsley, and next 5 ingredients in a bowl; stir well, and set aside.

Cut red pepper in half lengthwise; discard seeds and membranes. Place pepper, skin side up, on a foil-lined baking sheet; flatten with palm of hand. Broil 3 inches from heat 10 minutes or until blackened and charred. Place in a heavy-duty, zip-top plastic bag, and seal; let stand 15 minutes. Peel and discard skins, and cut pepper halves lengthwise into thin strips.

Combine beans and cumin in a bowl; stir well. Top each pita round evenly with eggplant mixture, red pepper strips, bean mixture, yogurt, and green onions. Sprinkle with coarsely ground pepper. Yield: 2 servings.

PER SERVING: 294 CALORIES (15% FROM FAT)
FAT 5.0G (SATURATED FAT 1.0G)
PROTEIN 11.6G CARBOHYDRATE 53.8G
CHOLESTEROL 3MG SODIUM 543MG

Roasted Vegetable Pita

Mediterranean Pitas

MEDITERRANEAN PITAS

1 (19-ounce) can garbanzo beans, undrained
2 tablespoons sliced green onions
2 tablespoons sesame seeds, toasted
1½ tablespoons lemon juice
⅛ teaspoon salt
⅛ teaspoon hot sauce
1 clove garlic, minced
8 (8-inch) pita bread rounds
8 green leaf lettuce leaves
2 cups alfalfa sprouts
1 medium cucumber, thinly sliced
½ cup plain nonfat yogurt

Drain beans, reserving 2 tablespoons liquid. Position knife blade in food processor bowl; add beans, reserved liquid, green onions, and next 5 ingredients. Process until smooth, scraping sides of processor bowl once.

Spread bean mixture evenly on top of pitas. Place 1 lettuce leaf on each pita. Divide alfalfa sprouts and cucumber evenly among pitas. Drizzle 1 tablespoon yogurt over cucumbers on each pita. Roll each pita toward center at bottom. Wrap bottom of each pita in wax paper or decorative tissue paper. Serve immediately. Yield: 8 servings.

PER SERVING: 298 CALORIES (11% FROM FAT)
FAT 3.7G (SATURATED FAT 0.5G)
PROTEIN 9.6G CARBOHYDRATE 53.5G
CHOLESTEROL 0MG SODIUM 586MG

Fat Alert

The Middle Eastern falafel can be the basis of a hearty vegetarian sandwich. It is traditionally prepared by deep-frying patties of seasoned ground garbanzo beans. These falafels will be lower in fat because the patties are pan-fried in a nonstick skillet with just a small amount of oil.

FALAFEL SANDWICHES

1 (15-ounce) can garbanzo beans, drained
½ cup chopped onion
¼ cup fine, dry breadcrumbs
1 tablespoon chopped fresh parsley
1 teaspoon ground cumin
½ teaspoon ground coriander
¼ teaspoon salt
⅛ teaspoon black pepper
⅛ teaspoon ground red pepper
2 cloves garlic
Vegetable cooking spray
2 teaspoons olive oil, divided
Tahini Sauce
2 (6-inch) pita bread rounds, cut in half
4 curly leaf lettuce leaves

Position knife blade in food processor bowl; add first 10 ingredients, and process until smooth. Divide mixture into 8 equal portions, shaping each into a 3-inch patty. Coat a large nonstick skillet with cooking spray; add 1½ teaspoons oil, and place over medium heat until hot. Add 4 patties to skillet; cook 2 minutes on each side or until lightly browned. Repeat procedure with remaining oil and patties.

Spread about 2 tablespoons Tahini Sauce evenly into each pita half; fill each half with 1 lettuce leaf and 2 falafel patties. Yield: 4 servings.

TAHINI SAUCE

½ cup plain nonfat yogurt
2 tablespoons commercial tahini (sesame seed paste)
1 teaspoon lemon juice
Dash of ground red pepper
1 clove garlic, minced

Combine all ingredients in a bowl; stir with a wire whisk until well blended. Cover and chill. Yield: ½ cup.

PER SERVING: 302 CALORIES (28% FROM FAT)
FAT 9.4G (SATURATED FAT 1.3G)
PROTEIN 12.8G CARBOHYDRATE 43.1G
CHOLESTEROL 2MG SODIUM 485MG

Fruit and Cheese Pitas

1 cup finely chopped unpeeled Red Delicious
   apple
1 cup finely chopped unpeeled Granny Smith
   apple
½ cup chopped seedless red grapes
⅓ cup (1⅓ ounces) diced reduced-fat sharp
   Cheddar cheese
3 tablespoons slivered almonds, toasted
¼ cup plain nonfat yogurt
1 tablespoon frozen apple juice concentrate,
   undiluted
1 tablespoon lime juice
1 tablespoon reduced-calorie mayonnaise
¼ teaspoon dried tarragon
2 (6-inch) pita bread rounds, cut in half
4 curly leaf lettuce leaves

Combine apples, grapes, cheese, and almonds in a bowl; toss gently, and set aside.

Combine yogurt, apple juice concentrate, lime juice, mayonnaise, and tarragon in a bowl; stir well. Pour over apple mixture; toss gently.

Line each pita half with a lettuce leaf. Spoon ¾ cup apple mixture into each half. Serve immediately. Yield: 4 servings.

Per Serving: 188 Calories (30% from Fat)
Fat 6.2g (Saturated Fat 1.7g)
Protein 6.8g Carbohydrate 27.9g
Cholesterol 8mg Sodium 218mg

Fruit and Cheese Pita

EGGPLANT AND FETA PITAS

16 (½-inch-thick) eggplant slices
Vegetable cooking spray
4 (6-inch) pita bread rounds, cut in half
8 (½-inch-thick) tomato slices
¼ cup (1 ounce) crumbled feta cheese with peppercorns
¼ cup chopped red onion
12 large fresh basil leaves, thinly sliced

Arrange eggplant in a single layer in a 13- x 9- x 2-inch baking dish coated with cooking spray. Cover; bake at 425° for 10 minutes. Turn eggplant; cook, uncovered, 10 minutes. Let cool slightly.

Fill each pita half with 2 eggplant slices, 1 tomato slice, ½ tablespoon cheese, ½ tablespoon onion, and sliced basil leaves. Yield: 4 servings.

PER SERVING: 190 CALORIES (17% FROM FAT)
FAT 3.5G (SATURATED FAT 1.4G)
PROTEIN 7.2G   CARBOHYDRATE 34.2G
CHOLESTEROL 6MG   SODIUM 311MG

BROILED TOMATO AND PESTO BAGELS

3 tablespoons fresh basil leaves
1 tablespoon fresh parsley leaves
1½ teaspoons water
1 teaspoon pine nuts
1 teaspoon olive oil
1 teaspoon lemon juice
½ teaspoon red wine vinegar
⅛ teaspoon garlic powder
Dash of salt
2 bagels, split and toasted
4 (½-inch-thick) slices large ripe tomato
¼ cup (1 ounce) shredded part-skim mozzarella cheese

Position knife blade in miniature food processor bowl; add first 9 ingredients. Process until smooth, scraping sides of processor bowl occasionally.

Spread basil mixture evenly on 4 bagel halves. Top each bagel half with a tomato slice, and sprinkle evenly with cheese. Place bagel halves on a baking sheet. Broil 5½ inches from heat (with electric oven door partially opened) 1 minute or until cheese melts. Yield: 2 servings.

PER SERVING: 251 CALORIES (23% FROM FAT)
FAT 6.5G (SATURATED FAT 2.0G)
PROTEIN 11.0G   CARBOHYDRATE 38.3G
CHOLESTEROL 8MG   SODIUM 459MG

OPEN-FACED VEGETABLE MELT

½ teaspoon olive oil
¼ cup thinly sliced onion
½ small zucchini, halved lengthwise and sliced (about ½ cup)
1 clove garlic, minced
½ cup seeded, coarsely chopped unpeeled tomato
¼ cup commercial roasted red bell peppers, drained and coarsely chopped
¼ teaspoon dried thyme
⅛ teaspoon pepper
½ cup (2 ounces) shredded provolone cheese
1 (5-inch) piece Italian bread, split lengthwise and toasted (about ¼ pound)
1 tablespoon grated Parmesan cheese

Heat oil in a medium-size nonstick skillet over medium heat. Add onion, zucchini, and garlic; sauté 5 minutes or until tender. Add tomato and next 3 ingredients; cook 1 minute.

Sprinkle 2 tablespoons provolone cheese over each bread half; top each half with ½ cup vegetable mixture. Sprinkle remaining ¼ cup provolone cheese and Parmesan cheese evenly over vegetable mixture. Broil 3 inches from heat (with electric oven door partially opened) 2 minutes or until cheese melts. Yield: 2 servings.

PER SERVING: 307 CALORIES (30% FROM FAT)
FAT 10.2G (SATURATED FAT 5.5G)
PROTEIN 14.7G   CARBOHYDRATE 39.2G
CHOLESTEROL 22MG   SODIUM 731MG

Bean and Vegetable Tortilla Stacks

BEAN AND VEGETABLE TORTILLA STACKS

1½ cups (6 ounces) shredded farmer cheese, divided
1 cup part-skim ricotta cheese
1 cup shredded carrot
½ cup chopped radish
¼ cup chopped ripe olives
1 (15-ounce) can garbanzo beans, drained
3 cloves garlic, halved
½ cup firmly packed fresh parsley sprigs
3 green onions, cut into ½-inch pieces
1 tablespoon lemon juice
½ teaspoon ground cumin
12 (6-inch) corn tortillas
Green or sweet red pepper rings (optional)
Red Chile Sauce

Combine 1 cup farmer cheese and next 4 ingredients; stir well, and set aside.

Position knife blade in food processor bowl; add garbanzo beans and garlic. Process bean mixture 1 minute or until smooth. Add parsley sprigs, green onions, lemon juice, and cumin; process 10 seconds or until onion is minced, scraping sides of processor bowl occasionally.

Place 4 tortillas on an ungreased baking sheet. Spread each with one-eighth of bean mixture; top with one-eighth of cheese mixture. Repeat with remaining tortillas, bean mixture, and cheese mixture, ending with remaining 4 tortillas. Sprinkle remaining ½ cup farmer cheese evenly over stacks. Bake at 375° for 15 minutes or until thoroughly heated. Cut each in half. Garnish with pepper rings, if desired. Serve with Red Chile Sauce. Yield: 8 servings.

RED CHILE SAUCE
1 large dried pasilla chile pepper
1 medium onion, quartered
4 cloves garlic, halved
1 (28-ounce) can plum tomatoes, drained
½ teaspoon ground cumin
¼ teaspoon hot sauce

Wash chile; remove stem, seeds, and veins. Place chile in a bowl; add boiling water to cover. Let stand 15 minutes or until chile is soft; drain and coarsely chop.

Position knife blade in food processor bowl; add chile, onion, and garlic. Pulse 4 or 5 times or until finely chopped. Add tomatoes, cumin, and hot sauce; process 1 minute or until smooth. Yield: 2 cups.

PER SERVING: 291 CALORIES (27% FROM FAT)
FAT 8.7G (SATURATED FAT 3.9G)
PROTEIN 17.5G CARBOHYDRATE 38.2G
CHOLESTEROL 23MG SODIUM 500MG

MINI MEXICAN PIZZAS

2 cups seeded, diced unpeeled tomato
1 tablespoon minced fresh cilantro
1 tablespoon finely chopped green onions
½ teaspoon ground cumin
⅛ teaspoon garlic powder
1 tablespoon fresh lime juice
6 (8-inch) flour tortillas
1½ cups fat-free refried beans
¾ cup (3 ounces) shredded reduced-fat Monterey Jack cheese

Combine first 6 ingredients in a bowl; stir well, and set aside.

Arrange tortillas on baking sheets, and bake at 400° for 2 minutes. Turn tortillas, and bake an additional minute. Spread ¼ cup beans over each tortilla; top with ⅓ cup tomato mixture and 2 tablespoons cheese. Bake at 400° for 6 minutes or until the tortillas are crisp and cheese melts; cut into wedges. Yield: 6 servings.

PER SERVING: 251 CALORIES (22% FROM FAT)
FAT 6.0G (SATURATED FAT 2.1G)
PROTEIN 12.2G CARBOHYDRATE 37.8G
CHOLESTEROL 9MG SODIUM 510MG

BROCCOLI-CHEESE CALZONES

1 package active dry yeast
1 cup warm water (105° to 115°), divided
¼ cup honey
¼ cup margarine, melted
¼ cup frozen egg substitute, thawed
2½ cups all-purpose flour, divided
1½ cups whole wheat flour
¾ teaspoon salt
2 tablespoons whole wheat flour
Vegetable cooking spray
Broccoli-Cheese Filling

Dissolve yeast in ¼ cup warm water in a large bowl; let stand 5 minutes. Combine remaining ¾ cup warm water, honey, margarine, and egg substitute; add to yeast mixture. Stir in 1 cup all-purpose flour, 1½ cups whole wheat flour, and salt. Stir in enough of the remaining 1½ cups all-purpose flour to make a soft dough.

Sprinkle 2 tablespoons whole wheat flour over work surface. Turn dough out onto floured surface; knead until smooth and elastic (about 8 to 10 minutes). Place dough in a bowl coated with cooking spray; turn to coat top. Cover and let rise in a warm place (85°), free from drafts, 1 hour or until doubled in bulk.

Punch dough down; divide into 10 equal portions. Roll each portion into a 6-inch circle. Spoon ⅓ cup Broccoli-Cheese Filling onto half of each circle, leaving a ½-inch border. Moisten edges; fold plain halves over filling. Crimp edges to seal. Place on baking sheets coated with cooking spray. Bake at 400° for 15 minutes or until golden. Yield: 10 servings.

BROCCOLI-CHEESE FILLING
1 (10-ounce) package frozen chopped broccoli, thawed
1 (15-ounce) carton light ricotta cheese
½ cup (2 ounces) shredded part-skim mozzarella cheese
¼ cup grated Parmesan cheese
½ teaspoon dried oregano

Cook broccoli according to package directions, omitting salt and fat. Drain; press between paper towels. Combine broccoli and remaining ingredients; stir well. Yield: 3⅓ cups.

PER SERVING: 312 CALORIES (25% FROM FAT)
FAT 8.5G (SATURATED FAT 2.9G)
PROTEIN 14.1G   CARBOHYDRATE 46.0G
CHOLESTEROL 12MG   SODIUM 341MG

SPINACH-CHEESE CALZONES WITH TOMATO SAUCE

1 (1-pound) loaf commercial frozen white bread dough
1 (10-ounce) package frozen chopped spinach, thawed and drained
Vegetable cooking spray
½ cup chopped onion
½ cup light ricotta cheese
½ cup (4 ounces) Neufchâtel-style cheese with herbs and spices
⅛ teaspoon pepper
1 egg, lightly beaten
1 cup seeded, chopped unpeeled tomato
¼ teaspoon salt
¼ teaspoon dried basil
¼ teaspoon dried oregano
1 (8-ounce) can no-salt-added tomato sauce

Thaw bread dough; set aside.

Press spinach between paper towels until barely moist; set aside.

Coat a medium skillet with cooking spray; place over medium heat until hot. Add onion; sauté 3 minutes or until tender. Remove from heat; add ricotta cheese and next 3 ingredients, stirring well. Add spinach, stirring well; remove from heat.

Divide dough into 8 equal portions. Working with 1 portion at a time (cover remaining portions to keep dough from drying out), roll each portion to ⅛-inch thickness. Place on a large baking sheet coated with cooking spray, and pat each portion

Spinach-Cheese Calzone with Tomato Sauce

into a 6-inch circle with floured fingertips. Spoon ¼ cup spinach mixture onto half of each circle; moisten edges of dough with water. Fold dough over filling; press edges together with a fork to seal. Lightly coat with cooking spray.

Bake at 375° for 20 minutes or until golden. Remove from oven, and lightly coat again with cooking spray; keep calzones warm. Combine tomato and next 4 ingredients in a small saucepan. Bring to a boil; reduce heat to medium, and cook 10 minutes. Serve calzones with sauce. Yield: 8 servings.

PER SERVING: 238 CALORIES (27% FROM FAT)
FAT 7.1G (SATURATED FAT 3.1G)
PROTEIN 10.5G   CARBOHYDRATE 34.6G
CHOLESTEROL 41MG   SODIUM 464MG

Fresh Pepper Pasta (recipe on page 90)

Grain & Pasta Entrées

*W*hether you are a full-time vegetarian or just occasionally choose a meatless meal, as a healthy eater you know the value of grains and pasta. In fact, health experts recommend six to eleven servings of rice, pasta, cereal (grains), or bread each day. What's so great about foods like rice, couscous, orzo, barley, and cornmeal? They contain a hefty load of complex carbohydrates along with valuable protein, vitamins, and minerals.

The best news is that these healthy ingredients are abundant in low-fat creations such as Italian Polenta (page 78), Vegetable Paella (page 84), and Fettuccine Primavera (page 86). Like all the recipes in this chapter, these contain at least 10 grams of protein per serving, enough for a complete meal. Try one of these dishes tonight!

BAKED BARLEY AND BEANS

Barley is high in soluble fiber (the type that can help lower blood cholesterol) and is a good source of B vitamins and protein.

1 cup pearl barley, uncooked
1¼ cups canned vegetable or chicken broth, undiluted
1¼ cups water
Vegetable cooking spray
2 cups sliced fresh mushrooms
1 cup chopped onion
½ cup diced green pepper
1 (15-ounce) can black beans, rinsed and drained
⅛ teaspoon salt
¼ teaspoon pepper
3 tablespoons sunflower kernels

Spread barley on a baking sheet; bake at 350° for 8 minutes or until lightly browned. Combine barley, vegetable broth, and water in a medium saucepan; bring to a boil. Cover, reduce heat, and simmer 20 minutes or until barley is tender and liquid is absorbed.

Coat a nonstick skillet with cooking spray; place over medium-high heat until hot. Add mushrooms, onion, and green pepper; sauté until tender. Stir in barley, beans, salt, and pepper; spoon mixture into a 1½-quart baking dish coated with cooking spray. Cover and bake at 350° for 30 minutes or until thoroughly heated. Sprinkle with sunflower kernels; bake, uncovered, an additional 5 minutes. Yield: 5 servings.

PER SERVING: 259 CALORIES (15% FROM FAT)
FAT 4.3G (SATURATED FAT 0.5G)
PROTEIN 10.1G   CARBOHYDRATE 47.7G
CHOLESTEROL 0MG   SODIUM 440MG

BULGUR PILAF-STUFFED CRÊPES

½ cup all-purpose flour
1 cup skim milk
3 egg whites
1 egg
Vegetable cooking spray
2 teaspoons olive oil
½ cup shredded carrot
¼ cup plus 2 tablespoons finely chopped onion
2 cloves garlic, minced
1⅔ cups water
1 cup canned vegetable broth, undiluted
1⅓ cups bulgur (cracked wheat), uncooked
½ cup freshly grated Parmesan cheese, divided
¼ cup plus 2 tablespoons minced fresh parsley
¼ cup pine nuts, toasted

Position knife blade in food processor bowl; add first 4 ingredients. Process 1 minute or until smooth, scraping sides of processor bowl occasionally. Chill batter 1 hour.

Coat a 7-inch crêpe pan or nonstick skillet with cooking spray; place over medium heat until hot. Pour 2½ tablespoons batter into pan; quickly tilt pan in all directions so batter covers pan in a thin film. Cook 1 minute or until crêpe can be shaken loose from pan. Flip crêpe, and cook about 30 seconds. Remove from pan; place crêpe on a towel to cool. Repeat until all batter is used. (Recipe makes about 12 crêpes.) Stack cooled crêpes between layers of wax paper to prevent sticking.

Heat olive oil in a nonstick skillet over medium-high heat until hot. Add carrot, onion, and minced garlic; sauté 3 minutes. Add water and broth; bring to a boil. Stir in bulgur; cover, reduce heat, and simmer 15 minutes or until bulgur is tender and liquid is absorbed. Stir in ¼ cup cheese, parsley, and pine nuts.

Spoon ⅓ cup bulgur mixture down center of each crêpe. Roll up crêpes; place in a 13- x 9- x 2-inch baking dish coated with cooking spray.

Sprinkle with remaining ¼ cup cheese. Bake at 375° for 30 minutes or until thoroughly heated. Yield: 6 servings.

PER SERVING: 286 CALORIES (27% FROM FAT)
FAT 8.7G (SATURATED FAT 2.6G)
PROTEIN 14.0G CARBOHYDRATE 41.1G
CHOLESTEROL 44MG SODIUM 344MG

CHICAGO DEEP-DISH VEGETABLE PIZZA

1 teaspoon sugar
1 package active dry yeast
1 cup warm water (105° to 115°)
2½ cups all-purpose flour
½ cup yellow cornmeal
¼ teaspoon salt
1 tablespoon olive oil
Vegetable cooking spray
1 tablespoon olive oil
1½ cups chopped green pepper
1½ cups chopped onion
1 garlic clove, crushed
2½ cups sliced fresh mushrooms
2 teaspoons dried oregano
¼ teaspoon salt
2 tablespoons yellow cornmeal
1½ cups canned crushed tomatoes
1¼ cups (5 ounces) shredded reduced-fat
    Monterey Jack cheese
¾ cup (3 ounces) shredded provolone cheese

Dissolve sugar and yeast in warm water in a small bowl; let stand 5 minutes. Place flour, ½ cup cornmeal, and ¼ teaspoon salt in food processor, and pulse 2 times or until blended. With processor on, slowly add yeast mixture and 1 tablespoon oil through food chute; process until dough forms a ball. Process for 1 additional minute.

Turn dough out onto a lightly floured surface, and knead lightly 4 or 5 times. Place dough in a bowl coated with cooking spray, turning to coat top. Cover and let rise in a warm place (85°), free from drafts, 45 minutes or until doubled in bulk.

Heat 1 tablespoon oil in a large nonstick skillet over medium heat. Add green pepper, onion, and crushed garlic, and sauté 5 minutes. Add mushrooms, oregano, and ¼ teaspoon salt; sauté 3 minutes or until tender. Remove from heat; let cool.

Punch dough down; cover and let rest 5 minutes. Divide dough in half. Roll each half into an 11-inch circle on a lightly floured surface. Coat 2 (9-inch) round cakepans with cooking spray, and sprinkle each with 1 tablespoon cornmeal. Place a circle of dough in each pan, and press dough up sides of pan. Cover and let rise 20 minutes or until puffy.

Spread half of vegetable mixture over each prepared crust, and top each with half of the crushed tomatoes. Sprinkle cheeses evenly over pizzas.

Bake at 475° for 15 minutes. Reduce temperature to 375°, and bake pizzas an additional 15 minutes. Cut each pizza into 4 wedges. Yield: 8 servings.

PER SERVING: 342 CALORIES (28% FROM FAT)
FAT 10.6G (SATURATED FAT 4.4G)
PROTEIN 14.8G CARBOHYDRATE 47.2G
CHOLESTEROL 19MG SODIUM 417MG

Heart Smart

For cardiovascular fitness, you need to exercise three times a week for 15 to 20 minutes at your target heart rate (number of beats per minute). Here's how you compute that target:
1. Subtract your age from 220. That's your maximum heart rate.
2. Multiply your maximum rate by 50 percent. That's the low end of your target heart rate.
3. Multiply your maximum rate by 75 percent. That's the high end of your target heart rate.

Take a break during exercise to check your pulse. The number of beats per minute should fall within your target range. If your pulse is lower than the target, exercise more strenuously. If it's higher, slow down.

SWEET PEPPER-CORN PIZZA WITH CORNMEAL CRUST

1¾ cups all-purpose flour, divided
½ cup plus 1 tablespoon yellow cornmeal,
    divided
¼ teaspoon salt
1 package active dry yeast
¾ cup very warm water (120° to 130°)
1 tablespoon olive oil
Vegetable cooking spray
2 cups thinly sliced purple onion, separated
    into rings
1 cup chopped sweet red pepper
2 teaspoons dried Italian seasoning
¼ teaspoon dried crushed red pepper
1 clove garlic, minced
1⅔ cups frozen whole kernel corn, thawed
¼ teaspoon salt
1 cup (4 ounces) shredded Monterey Jack
    cheese, divided

Combine 1¼ cups flour, ½ cup cornmeal, ¼ teaspoon salt, and yeast in a large bowl; stir well. Add water and oil; beat at medium speed of an electric mixer 2 minutes. Stir in ½ cup flour to make a soft dough. Turn dough out onto a lightly floured surface; knead until smooth and elastic. Cover; let rest 20 minutes. Coat a 15- x 10- x 1-inch jellyroll pan with cooking spray, and sprinkle with remaining 1 tablespoon cornmeal. Roll dough to a 15- x 10-inch rectangle; place in prepared pan.

Coat a large nonstick skillet with cooking spray; place over medium-high heat until hot. Add onion and next 4 ingredients; sauté 7 minutes. Remove from heat; stir in corn and ¼ teaspoon salt.

Sprinkle ½ cup cheese over prepared crust. Spread onion mixture evenly over cheese; top with remaining cheese. Bake at 400° for 20 minutes or until golden. Yield: 6 servings.

PER SERVING: 332 CALORIES (24% FROM FAT)
FAT 8.9G (SATURATED FAT 4.0G)
PROTEIN 11.9G   CARBOHYDRATE 52.3G
CHOLESTEROL 15MG   SODIUM 303MG

ITALIAN POLENTA

If you can't find precooked polenta, cook ¾ cup dry polenta in 2¼ cups water to make the amount needed in this recipe. Regular dry polenta cooks in about 30 minutes.

Vegetable cooking spray
1 cup finely chopped zucchini (about 1 small)
1 cup frozen whole kernel corn, thawed
1 (8-ounce) can no-salt-added tomato sauce
¾ cup finely chopped onion
1 teaspoon dried sage
1 teaspoon dried Italian seasoning
⅛ teaspoon salt
⅛ teaspoon garlic powder
2 teaspoons balsamic vinegar
½ (32-ounce) package precooked polenta
    (yellow cornmeal)
1 cup (4 ounces) shredded part-skim
    mozzarella cheese

Coat a medium nonstick skillet with cooking spray; place over medium-high heat until hot. Add zucchini and next 7 ingredients. Reduce heat, and cook 5 minutes or until vegetables are tender. Stir in vinegar. Set aside, and keep warm.

Cut precooked polenta crosswise into 12 even slices; place on a baking sheet, and bake at 350° for 10 to 15 minutes or until thoroughly heated. Arrange 3 polenta slices on each serving plate. Top each serving with ⅓ cup sauce and ¼ cup mozzarella cheese. Yield: 4 servings.

PER SERVING: 241 CALORIES (23% FROM FAT)
FAT 6.1G (SATURATED FAT 3.1G)
PROTEIN 11.6G   CARBOHYDRATE 37.6G
CHOLESTEROL 16MG   SODIUM 231MG

Italian Polenta

WHITE BEAN-POLENTA PIE

½ pound fennel
2 cups water
¼ teaspoon salt
⅔ cup instant polenta
Vegetable cooking spray
1 teaspoon olive oil
¾ cup finely chopped carrot
¾ cup finely chopped onion
2 cloves garlic, crushed
2 (15-ounce) cans cannellini beans, drained
½ teaspoon rubbed sage
¼ teaspoon ground red pepper
1 cup (4 ounces) shredded provolone cheese

Wash fennel; trim off leaves, and mince, reserving 2 tablespoons. Trim off tough outer stalks, and discard. Cut bulb in half lengthwise; remove and discard core. Cut bulb crosswise into ¼-inch slices, reserving ¾ cup. Reserve remaining fennel leaves and bulb for other uses.

Combine water and salt in a 10-inch cast-iron skillet; bring to a boil. Add polenta in a slow, steady stream, stirring constantly. Reduce heat; cook, uncovered, 5 minutes or until mixture pulls away from sides of skillet, stirring constantly. Remove from heat, and spread evenly in skillet. Let stand 5 minutes.

Coat a large nonstick skillet with cooking spray; add olive oil. Place over medium heat until hot. Add ¾ cup fennel, carrot, onion, and garlic; sauté until tender. Stir in beans, 2 tablespoons fennel leaves, sage, and red pepper.

Spoon bean mixture evenly over polenta; sprinkle with cheese. Bake at 400° for 12 to 15 minutes or until thoroughly heated and cheese melts. Let stand 15 minutes before serving. Yield: 6 servings.

PER SERVING: 217 CALORIES (27% FROM FAT)
FAT 6.6G (SATURATED FAT 3.4G)
PROTEIN 10.8G CARBOHYDRATE 27.9G
CHOLESTEROL 13MG SODIUM 472MG

GREEN CHILE-RICE CASSEROLE

1 tablespoon reduced-calorie stick margarine
½ cup chopped onion
1 cup plus 2 tablespoons canned vegetable or chicken broth, undiluted
1 cup plus 2 tablespoons water
1 (4-ounce) can chopped green chiles, undrained
1 jalapeño pepper, seeded and minced
1 cup long-grain rice, uncooked
1 cup (4 ounces) shredded reduced-fat Monterey Jack cheese, divided
1 (8-ounce) carton nonfat sour cream
1 (2-ounce) jar diced pimiento, drained
⅛ teaspoon garlic powder
Dash of salt
Vegetable cooking spray
Fresno pepper slices (optional)
Fresh cilantro sprig (optional)

Melt margarine in a large saucepan over medium-high heat. Add onion, and sauté until tender.

Add vegetable broth and next 3 ingredients. Bring to a boil; add rice, stirring well. Cover, reduce heat, and simmer 25 minutes or until rice is tender and liquid is absorbed. Add ⅔ cup cheese and next 4 ingredients to rice mixture, stirring well.

Spoon rice mixture into a 1-quart baking dish coated with cooking spray. Bake, uncovered, at 350° for 20 minutes. Sprinkle with remaining ⅓ cup cheese. Bake an additional 5 minutes or until cheese melts. If desired, garnish with pepper slices and a cilantro sprig. Yield: 4 (1-cup) servings.

PER SERVING: 335 CALORIES (22% FROM FAT)
FAT 8.1G (SATURATED FAT 3.3G)
PROTEIN 16.4G CARBOHYDRATE 47.0G
CHOLESTEROL 19MG SODIUM 566MG

Green Chile-Rice Casserole

Bean- and Rice-Stuffed Peppers

BEAN- AND RICE-STUFFED PEPPERS

6 medium-size sweet red, yellow, or orange
    peppers
1½ cups cooked long-grain rice (cooked
    without salt or fat)
½ cup chopped onion
1 (15-ounce) can red kidney beans, rinsed and
    drained
1 (14½-ounce) can no-salt-added stewed
    tomatoes
1 (4-ounce) can chopped green chiles, drained
1 teaspoon chili powder
1½ cups (6 ounces) shredded reduced-fat
    sharp Cheddar cheese, divided

Cut tops off peppers, and remove seeds. Cook
tops and bottoms of peppers in boiling water 5
minutes. Drain peppers; set aside.
    Combine rice and next 5 ingredients in a medium
bowl; stir in 1 cup cheese. Spoon mixture evenly
into peppers, and replace pepper tops; place peppers in an 11- x 7- x 1½-inch baking dish. Add hot
water to dish to a depth of ½ inch.
    Bake, uncovered, at 350° for 25 minutes. Remove
pepper tops, and sprinkle stuffed peppers evenly
with remaining ½ cup cheese. Replace tops, and
bake an additional 5 minutes or until cheese melts.
Yield: 6 servings.

PER SERVING: 257 CALORIES (22% FROM FAT)
FAT 6.3G (SATURATED FAT 3.3G)
PROTEIN 15.4G CARBOHYDRATE 36.8G
CHOLESTEROL 19MG SODIUM 336MG

GREEK WHITE BEAN RISOTTO

*Arborio rice has shorter, fatter kernels than regular
rice. It can be found with other kinds of rice in large
supermarkets, and it may be labeled Italian risotto.*

4½ cups water
Vegetable cooking spray
1 tablespoon minced garlic
8 ounces Arborio rice, uncooked
1 teaspoon dried oregano
¾ cup canned Great Northern beans, drained
¼ cup diced sun-dried tomato
¼ cup sliced ripe olives
1 (4-ounce) package feta cheese with basil and
    tomato, finely crumbled
¼ cup freshly grated Parmesan cheese

Pour water into a medium saucepan; place over
medium heat. Cover and bring to a simmer; reduce
heat to low, and keep warm. (Do not boil.)
    Coat a large saucepan with cooking spray; place
over medium-high heat until hot. Add garlic; sauté
1 minute. Add rice and oregano; reduce heat to
medium-low. Add 1 cup simmering water, stirring
constantly until most of liquid is absorbed. Repeat
procedure, adding ½ cup water at a time. After 15
minutes, stir in beans, tomato, and olives. Continue
to add water, ½ cup at a time, stirring constantly
until liquid is absorbed, about 25 minutes. (Rice
will be tender and have a creamy consistency.) Add
cheeses; stir until melted. Yield: 5 servings.
    Note: Regular feta cheese may be substituted for
basil-tomato cheese.

PER SERVING: 299 CALORIES (23% FROM FAT)
FAT 7.7G (SATURATED FAT 4.6G)
PROTEIN 11.2G CARBOHYDRATE 46.2G
CHOLESTEROL 24MG SODIUM 570MG

VEGETABLE PAELLA

½ cup boiling water
¼ teaspoon threads of saffron
Vegetable cooking spray
1 teaspoon olive oil
2 tablespoons minced garlic
¾ cup sliced green onions
¾ cup diced sweet red pepper
1 (9-ounce) package frozen artichoke hearts,
     thawed and quartered
1½ cups water
1½ cups canned vegetable or chicken broth,
     undiluted
1½ cups long-grain brown rice, uncooked
1 cup canned no-salt-added whole tomatoes,
     drained and chopped
2 teaspoons Hungarian sweet paprika
1 (15-ounce) can cannellini beans, drained
1 cup thinly sliced arugula
¾ cup frozen English peas, thawed
½ cup freshly grated Parmesan cheese
½ teaspoon freshly ground pepper

Combine boiling water and saffron; cover and let stand 10 minutes.

Coat a large saucepan with cooking spray; add olive oil. Place over medium-high heat until hot. Add garlic, and sauté 1 minute. Add green onions, red pepper, and artichoke hearts; sauté 5 minutes.

Stir in saffron water, 1½ cups water, vegetable broth, brown rice, tomatoes, and paprika. Bring to a boil; cover, reduce heat, and simmer 15 minutes. Stir in cannellini beans, arugula, and peas; cover and cook 15 to 20 minutes or until liquid is absorbed and rice is tender. Remove from heat, and let stand 5 minutes. Spoon into a serving bowl; sprinkle with Parmesan cheese and ground pepper. Yield: 6 servings.

PER SERVING: 337 CALORIES (15% FROM FAT)
FAT 5.7G (SATURATED FAT 2.1G)
PROTEIN 14.2G CARBOHYDRATE 59.1G
CHOLESTEROL 6MG SODIUM 615MG

BROWN RICE WITH GARDEN VEGETABLES AND BEANS

2 teaspoons olive oil
1 cup chopped onion
3 cloves garlic, minced
⅔ cup water
⅔ cup canned vegetable or chicken broth,
     undiluted
1 cup instant brown rice, uncooked
1 cup sliced carrot
¾ cup chopped tomato
1 teaspoon dried thyme
½ teaspoon dried oregano
¼ teaspoon salt
¼ teaspoon pepper
½ pound fresh asparagus
1 cup sliced zucchini
1 (15-ounce) can no-salt-added garbanzo
     beans, drained
¼ cup grated Asiago or Parmesan cheese

Heat oil in a large saucepan over medium-high heat until hot. Add onion and garlic; sauté until onion is tender.

Add water and broth to onion mixture, and bring to a boil. Stir in rice and next 6 ingredients. Cover, reduce heat, and simmer 10 minutes or until rice is tender and liquid is absorbed. Let stand, covered, 5 minutes.

Snap off tough ends of asparagus. Remove scales from stalks with a knife or vegetable peeler, if desired. Cut spears into 1-inch pieces. Arrange asparagus and zucchini in a vegetable steamer over boiling water. Cover and steam 8 minutes or until vegetables are crisp-tender. Drain; add to rice mixture. Add beans and cheese; toss gently. Yield: 4 servings.

PER SERVING: 318 CALORIES (21% FROM FAT)
FAT 7.3G (SATURATED FAT 1.8G)
PROTEIN 13.9G CARBOHYDRATE 53.1G
CHOLESTEROL 5MG SODIUM 407MG

JICAMA BURRITOS

Vegetable cooking spray
2 teaspoons vegetable oil
1 cup peeled, diced jicama
1 cup chopped onion
1 teaspoon cumin seeds
1½ cups cooked brown rice (cooked without
    salt or fat)
1¼ cups (5 ounces) shredded reduced-fat
    Cheddar cheese
1 cup shredded carrot
½ cup seeded, diced tomato
6 (8-inch) flour tortillas
½ cup commercial no-salt-added salsa
¾ cup nonfat sour cream

Coat a medium nonstick skillet with cooking spray; add oil. Place over medium heat until hot. Add jicama, and sauté 3 minutes. Add onion and cumin seeds; sauté 5 minutes or until vegetables are tender. Remove from heat; stir in brown rice, cheese, carrot, and tomato.

Spoon jicama mixture evenly down center of each tortilla. Roll up tortillas, and place seam side down in a 13- x 9- x 2-inch baking pan coated with cooking spray. Cover and bake at 425° for 15 minutes or until thoroughly heated.

Transfer to individual serving plates. Top each with 1 tablespoon plus 1 teaspoon salsa and 2 tablespoons sour cream. Serve immediately. Yield: 6 servings.

PER SERVING: 271 CALORIES (28% FROM FAT)
FAT 8.5G (SATURATED FAT 3.3G)
PROTEIN 13.4G CARBOHYDRATE 34.7G
CHOLESTEROL 15MG SODIUM 376MG

CHEESE TORTELLINI WITH HERBED TOMATO SAUCE

Vegetable cooking spray
½ cup minced onion
½ cup diced celery
½ cup diced carrot
2 cloves garlic, minced
1 (14½-ounce) can no-salt-added whole
    tomatoes, undrained and finely chopped
2 tablespoons minced fresh oregano
2 tablespoons minced fresh basil
2 (9-ounce) packages fresh cheese tortellini,
    uncooked
Fresh basil sprigs (optional)

Coat a nonstick skillet with cooking spray; place over medium-high heat until hot. Add onion, celery, carrot, and garlic; sauté 5 minutes or until onion is tender. Add tomato, oregano, and basil; reduce heat, and simmer, uncovered, 20 minutes or until thickened.

Cook tortellini according to package directions, omitting salt and fat; drain well.

For each serving, top ¾ cup tortellini with ⅔ cup sauce. Garnish with basil sprigs, if desired. Yield: 6 servings.

PER SERVING: 280 CALORIES (14% FROM FAT)
FAT 4.2G (SATURATED FAT 2.1G)
PROTEIN 15.0G CARBOHYDRATE 61.7G
CHOLESTEROL 38MG SODIUM 406MG

FYI

Freezing leftover fresh herbs is easy and requires no blanching. Wash the herbs gently, and freeze them while still wet. Short clippings, with leaves still on the stem, can be placed in small zip-top plastic freezer bags. Herbs, such as parsley and chives, can be washed, patted dry, and chopped before they are frozen. Frozen herbs are great for cooking but not for garnishing.

FETTUCCINE PRIMAVERA

3 quarts water
1 (8-ounce) package fettuccine, uncooked
¾ cup evaporated skimmed milk
½ cup small fresh broccoli flowerets
¼ cup grated Parmesan cheese
¼ cup finely chopped onion
1 teaspoon olive oil
½ teaspoon garlic powder
½ teaspoon dried basil
¼ teaspoon salt
⅛ teaspoon pepper
½ cup diced unpeeled tomato

Bring 3 quarts water to a boil in a large saucepan; add pasta, and cook 7 minutes. Drain well, and return to saucepan. Add milk and next 8 ingredients; place over medium heat, and cook 7 minutes or until thickened and bubbly. Stir in tomato. Serve immediately. Yield: 4 (1-cup) servings.

PER SERVING: 294 CALORIES (12% FROM FAT)
FAT 3.8G (SATURATED FAT 1.3G)
PROTEIN 13.7G CARBOHYDRATE 50.9G
CHOLESTEROL 6MG SODIUM 304MG

LINGUINE WITH BASIL-ONION SAUCE

1 tablespoon olive oil
4 cups thinly sliced yellow onion
½ teaspoon salt
2 cloves garlic, minced
¼ cup dry white wine
1 (9-ounce) package fresh spinach or plain
    linguine
⅓ cup chopped fresh basil
3 tablespoons chopped walnuts, toasted
⅛ to ¼ teaspoon pepper
1 ounce chèvre (mild goat cheese), crumbled

Heat olive oil in a large skillet over medium heat. Add onion and salt; stir well. Cover and cook 15 minutes, stirring occasionally. Stir in garlic; cook, uncovered, 15 minutes or until onion turns deep golden, stirring frequently. Add wine; simmer 3 minutes, stirring occasionally. Remove from heat; set aside, and keep warm.

Cook pasta according to package directions, omitting salt and fat. Drain pasta, reserving ¼ cup cooking liquid. Add cooking liquid, pasta, basil, and remaining ingredients to onion mixture; toss well. Serve immediately. Yield: 4 (1¼-cup) servings.

PER SERVING: 376 CALORIES (22% FROM FAT)
FAT 9.4G (SATURATED FAT 1.9G)
PROTEIN 12.0G CARBOHYDRATE 59.3G
CHOLESTEROL 6MG SODIUM 381MG

MACARONI AND CHEESE

4 cups cooked elbow macaroni (about 2 cups
    uncooked), cooked without salt or fat
2 cups (8 ounces) shredded reduced-fat sharp
    Cheddar cheese
1 cup 1% low-fat cottage cheese
¾ cup nonfat sour cream
½ cup skim milk
2 tablespoons grated fresh onion
1½ teaspoons reduced-calorie stick margarine,
    melted
¼ teaspoon salt
¼ teaspoon pepper
1 egg, lightly beaten
Vegetable cooking spray
¼ cup dry breadcrumbs
1 tablespoon reduced-calorie stick margarine,
    melted
¼ teaspoon paprika
Fresh oregano sprigs (optional)

Combine first 10 ingredients; stir well, and spoon into a 2-quart baking dish coated with cooking spray. Combine breadcrumbs, margarine, and paprika; stir well. Sprinkle over casserole. Cover and bake at 350° for 30 minutes. Uncover; bake 5 minutes or until set. Garnish with oregano sprigs, if desired. Yield: 6 (1-cup) servings.

PER SERVING: 356 CALORIES (28% FROM FAT)
FAT 11.2G (SATURATED FAT 5.2G)
PROTEIN 24.9G CARBOHYDRATE 37.5G
CHOLESTEROL 63MG SODIUM 626MG

Macaroni and Cheese

Fresh Tomato Spaghetti

Fresh Tomato Spaghetti

Olive oil-flavored vegetable cooking spray
1¾ cups sliced fresh mushrooms
½ cup minced shallots
6 cups peeled, seeded, and chopped tomato
1½ cups no-salt-added tomato juice
1 (6-ounce) can no-salt-added tomato paste
2 tablespoons chopped fresh basil
2 teaspoons chopped fresh oregano
½ teaspoon fennel seeds
¼ teaspoon salt
1 bay leaf
12 ounces spaghetti, uncooked
Fresh oregano sprigs (optional)

Coat a large Dutch oven with cooking spray. Place over medium-high heat until hot. Add mushrooms and shallots; sauté until tender.

Add chopped tomato and next 7 ingredients, stirring well. Bring mixture to a boil; reduce heat, and simmer, uncovered, 40 minutes, stirring occasionally. Remove and discard bay leaf.

Cook pasta according to package directions, omitting salt and fat. Drain. Place on a serving platter, and top with tomato mixture. Garnish with oregano sprigs, if desired. Yield: 6 servings.

PER SERVING: 305 CALORIES (6% FROM FAT)
FAT 1.9G (SATURATED FAT 0.2G)
PROTEIN 11.5G CARBOHYDRATE 63.6G
CHOLESTEROL 0MG SODIUM 141MG

Ratatouille with Pasta and Feta

1 teaspoon olive oil
2 cups sliced leeks
3 cloves garlic, minced
½ teaspoon fennel seeds, crushed
2 cups sliced zucchini
¼ teaspoon salt
2 large sweet red peppers (about 1 pound), seeded and cut into thin strips
1½ cups chopped tomato
½ cup no-salt-added vegetable juice
12 ounces penne (short tubular pasta), uncooked
½ cup sliced fresh basil
3 ounces feta cheese, crumbled

Heat oil in a large nonstick skillet over medium-high heat until hot. Add leeks, garlic, and fennel seeds; sauté 5 minutes or until leeks are tender. Add zucchini and salt; sauté 3 minutes.

Stir in red pepper strips, chopped tomato, and vegetable juice; bring to a boil. Cover, reduce heat, and simmer 15 minutes, stirring occasionally.

Cook pasta according to package directions, omitting salt and fat; drain and place in a bowl. Add vegetable mixture; toss gently. Sprinkle with basil and cheese. Serve immediately. Yield: 6 servings.

PER SERVING: 308 CALORIES (15% FROM FAT)
FAT 5.2G (SATURATED FAT 2.4G)
PROTEIN 11.4G CARBOHYDRATE 54.7G
CHOLESTEROL 13MG SODIUM 278MG

FYI

Tomatoes come in varying shades of red as well as yellow and a seldom-seen white. There are also green tomatoes (for frying), which are simply tomatoes that haven't yet ripened. Medium to large round red tomatoes are perfect for slicing and chopping, as well as for serving cooked.

The tiny round shape of a cherry tomato is familiar in salads and as a garnish. Becoming more readily available are teardrop (or pear) and Roma (or plum) tomatoes. Teardrop tomatoes add an interesting shape to salads, while chopped Romas are good in salads and cooked sauces.

FRESH PEPPER PASTA

(pictured on page 74)

4 medium-size sweet red peppers (about 1½ pounds), seeded and chopped
2 tablespoons dry white wine
¾ cup drained canned navy beans
½ cup thinly sliced green onions
¼ cup plus 2 tablespoons shredded fresh basil leaves
1 tablespoon minced fresh oregano
1 tablespoon chopped ripe olives
6 ounces rotini (corkscrew pasta), uncooked
¼ cup plus 2 tablespoons (1½ ounces) grated Asiago cheese
1 tablespoon pine nuts, toasted
Fresh basil sprigs (optional)

Combine red pepper and wine in a saucepan; bring to a boil. Cover, reduce heat, and simmer 3 minutes.

Stir in beans and next 4 ingredients; bring to a boil. Cover, reduce heat, and simmer 10 minutes. Uncover; simmer 20 minutes, stirring occasionally.

Cook pasta according to package directions, omitting salt and fat. Drain well.

Place pasta on individual serving plates. Top with pepper mixture, cheese, and pine nuts. Garnish with basil sprigs, if desired. Yield: 3 (2-cup) servings.

PER SERVING: 378 CALORIES (18% FROM FAT)
FAT 7.6G (SATURATED FAT 2.5G)
PROTEIN 17.0G CARBOHYDRATE 63.0G
CHOLESTEROL 7MG SODIUM 392MG

Did You Know?

Asiago is an Italian cheese with a rich, nutty flavor. Young Asiago cheese can be sliced and eaten out of hand. As the cheese ages, it hardens and can then be grated. Parmesan cheese is a suitable substitute for Asiago in most recipes.

VERMICELLI WITH MUSHROOMS AND PINE NUTS

2 teaspoons margarine
2½ cups sliced fresh mushrooms
½ cup chopped onion
2 tablespoons all-purpose flour
1 cup evaporated skimmed milk
½ cup frozen English peas, thawed
¼ cup sliced green onions
1 (8-ounce) package vermicelli, uncooked
¼ cup freshly grated Parmesan cheese
2 tablespoons pine nuts, toasted
Freshly ground pepper (optional)

Melt margarine in a large nonstick skillet over medium heat. Add mushrooms and chopped onion; sauté until tender.

Add flour; cook, stirring constantly, 1 minute. Gradually add milk, stirring constantly. Cook, stirring constantly, until thickened and bubbly. Add peas and green onions; cook over medium-low heat, stirring constantly, 1 minute or until heated.

Cook vermicelli according to package directions, omitting salt and fat; drain. Combine vermicelli, mushroom mixture, cheese, pine nuts, and pepper, if desired, in a serving bowl; toss gently. Serve immediately. Yield: 4 (1½-cup) servings.

Note: Mushroom sauce may be cooked in the microwave. Place margarine and chopped onion in a 2-quart microwave-safe bowl. Cover with wax paper. Microwave at HIGH 2 minutes, stirring after 1 minute. Add mushrooms; cover with wax paper. Microwave at HIGH 2 minutes. Add flour, stirring well. Gradually stir in milk. Microwave at HIGH 3 to 4 minutes or until sauce is thickened and bubbly, stirring every minute. Add peas and green onions. Microwave at HIGH 1 minute or until thoroughly heated. Cook vermicelli according to package directions, and continue as directed above.

PER SERVING: 375 CALORIES (16% FROM FAT)
FAT 6.8G (SATURATED FAT 2.1G)
PROTEIN 18.2G CARBOHYDRATE 60.2G
CHOLESTEROL 7MG SODIUM 242MG

Vermicelli with Mushrooms and Pine Nuts

VEGETABLE CANNELLONI

1 (14½-ounce) can no-salt-added whole
   tomatoes, undrained
1 (8-ounce) can no-salt-added tomato sauce
2 tablespoons no-salt-added tomato paste
¼ cup finely chopped green pepper
¼ cup finely chopped shallots
1 clove garlic, crushed
½ teaspoon dried basil
Vegetable cooking spray
1 cup shredded carrot
1 cup shredded zucchini
½ cup diced fresh mushrooms
2 tablespoons chopped fresh parsley
2 cups 1% low-fat cottage cheese
¼ cup frozen egg substitute, thawed
2 tablespoons grated Parmesan cheese
½ teaspoon dried basil
⅛ teaspoon ground nutmeg
⅛ teaspoon ground white pepper
8 cannelloni shells (cooked without salt or fat)

Place tomatoes in container of an electric blender or food processor; cover and process until smooth. Transfer tomato puree to a saucepan; stir in tomato sauce and next 5 ingredients. Bring to a boil; reduce heat, and simmer, uncovered, 20 minutes, stirring occasionally. Spread ½ cup tomato mixture in an 11- x 7- x 1½-inch baking dish coated with cooking spray; set aside. Reserve remaining tomato mixture.

Coat a large nonstick skillet with cooking spray; place over medium-high heat until hot. Add carrot and next 3 ingredients; sauté until crisp-tender. Drain vegetable mixture well on paper towels.

Combine cottage cheese and next 5 ingredients in container of electric blender or food processor. Cover and process until mixture is smooth. Combine vegetable mixture and cheese mixture in a large bowl; stir well.

Spoon vegetable-cheese mixture into cannelloni shells; place in baking dish. Spoon remaining tomato mixture evenly over shells. Cover and bake at 375° for 20 minutes or until heated. Yield: 4 servings.

PER SERVING: 330 CALORIES (8% FROM FAT)
FAT 3.1G (SATURATED FAT 1.3G)
PROTEIN 24.5G CARBOHYDRATE 50.1G
CHOLESTEROL 6MG SODIUM 569MG

ARTICHOKE- AND SPINACH-STUFFED SHELLS

1 (10-ounce) package frozen chopped spinach,
   thawed
1 cup frozen artichoke hearts, thawed
12 jumbo pasta shells, uncooked
1 cup light ricotta cheese
2 tablespoons chopped fresh basil
1 tablespoon chopped fresh parsley
¼ teaspoon salt
2 tablespoons lemon juice
⅓ cup nonfat sour cream
2 (14½-ounce) cans no-salt-added stewed
   tomatoes, undrained and chopped
2 tablespoons cornstarch
1½ tablespoons chopped fresh basil
Vegetable cooking spray
Fresh basil sprigs (optional)

Cook spinach and artichoke hearts according to package directions, omitting salt; drain well. Chop artichoke hearts, and set aside.

Cook pasta shells according to package directions, omitting salt and fat; drain and set aside.

Position knife blade in food processor bowl; add spinach, ricotta cheese, and next 4 ingredients. Process 30 seconds or until smooth. Transfer to a bowl; stir in chopped artichokes and sour cream.

Combine tomatoes, cornstarch, and 1½ tablespoons basil in a saucepan; stir well. Cook over medium heat until thickened, stirring frequently. Spoon 1 cup tomato mixture in bottom of an 11- x 7- x 1½-inch baking dish coated with cooking spray.

Spoon spinach mixture evenly into shells. Arrange shells in baking dish. Pour remaining tomato mixture over shells. Bake, uncovered, at 350° for 30 minutes or until bubbly. Garnish with basil sprigs, if desired. Yield: 6 servings.

PER SERVING: 185 CALORIES (10% FROM FAT)
FAT 2.1G (SATURATED FAT 0.9G)
PROTEIN 11.2G CARBOHYDRATE 32.9G
CHOLESTEROL 5MG SODIUM 206MG

Artichoke- and Spinach-Stuffed Shells

Four-Cheese Vegetable Lasagna

FOUR-CHEESE VEGETABLE LASAGNA

1 (10-ounce) package frozen chopped spinach, thawed
Vegetable cooking spray
2 teaspoons vegetable oil
2 cups chopped fresh broccoli
1½ cups thinly sliced carrot
1 cup sliced green onions
½ cup chopped sweet red pepper
3 cloves garlic, crushed
½ cup all-purpose flour
3 cups 1% low-fat milk
½ cup freshly grated Parmesan cheese, divided
¼ teaspoon salt
¼ teaspoon pepper
1½ cups 1% low-fat cottage cheese
1 cup (4 ounces) shredded part-skim mozzarella cheese
½ cup (2 ounces) shredded Swiss cheese
12 cooked lasagna noodles (cooked without salt or fat)

Press spinach between paper towels until barely moist, and set aside. Coat a Dutch oven with cooking spray; add oil, and place over medium heat until hot. Add broccoli and next 4 ingredients; sauté 7 minutes. Set aside.

Place flour in a medium saucepan. Gradually add milk, stirring with a wire whisk until blended. Bring to a boil over medium heat, and cook 5 minutes or until thickened, stirring constantly. Add ¼ cup Parmesan cheese, salt, and pepper; cook an additional 1 minute, stirring constantly. Remove from heat; stir in spinach. Reserve ½ cup spinach mixture to spread over top layer of noodles; set aside.

Combine cottage cheese, mozzarella, and Swiss cheese; stir well. Spread ½ cup remaining spinach mixture in bottom of a 13- x 9- x 2-inch baking dish coated with cooking spray. Arrange 4 lasagna noodles over spinach mixture; top with half of cottage cheese mixture, half of vegetable mixture, and half of remaining spinach mixture. Repeat layers, ending with noodles. Spread reserved ½ cup spinach mixture over noodles, and sprinkle with remaining ¼ cup Parmesan cheese. Cover and bake at 375° for 35 minutes. Let stand 5 minutes before serving. Yield: 9 servings.

PER SERVING: 299 CALORIES (26% FROM FAT)
FAT 8.5G (SATURATED FAT 4.5G)
PROTEIN 20.4G CARBOHYDRATE 35.6G
CHOLESTEROL 22MG SODIUM 474MG

LAYERED VEGETABLE LASAGNA
(pictured on cover)

1 (10-ounce) package frozen chopped spinach, thawed and drained
1 (12-ounce) carton 1% low-fat cottage cheese
¼ cup egg substitute
Vegetable cooking spray
2 teaspoons olive oil
¾ cup minced onion
1 cup sliced fresh mushrooms
2 cloves garlic, minced
2 (14½-ounce) cans no-salt-added tomatoes, drained and chopped
¼ cup minced fresh parsley
¼ cup dry red wine
¼ cup no-salt-added tomato paste
2 teaspoons dried basil
1½ teaspoons dried oregano
1 teaspoon brown sugar
½ teaspoon pepper
¼ teaspoon salt
6 lasagna noodles, uncooked
5 cups thinly sliced zucchini (about 1¼ pounds)
1½ cups (6 ounces) finely shredded part-skim mozzarella cheese
2 tablespoons freshly grated Parmesan cheese

Press spinach between paper towels until barely moist. Combine spinach, cottage cheese, and egg substitute in a medium bowl; stir well, and set aside.

Coat a large saucepan with cooking spray; add oil, and place over medium-high heat until hot. Add onion, and sauté 3 minutes or until tender. Add mushrooms and garlic; sauté 2 minutes or until mushrooms are tender. Add tomatoes and next 8 ingredients; stir well. Reduce heat, and simmer, uncovered, 20 minutes. Remove tomato mixture from heat; set aside.

Coat a 13- x 9- x 2-inch baking dish with cooking spray. Spoon one-third of tomato mixture into baking dish. Arrange 3 uncooked noodles lengthwise in a single layer over tomato mixture; top with 1¼ cups spinach mixture. Layer 2½ cups zucchini over spinach, and sprinkle with ½ cup mozzarella cheese. Repeat layers; top with remaining tomato mixture. Cover and chill 8 hours.

Cover baking dish, and bake at 350° for 1 hour 30 minutes. Uncover and sprinkle with remaining ½ cup mozzarella cheese and Parmesan cheese. Cover and let stand 5 minutes before serving. Yield: 6 servings.

PER SERVING: 289 CALORIES (26% FROM FAT)
FAT 8.2G (SATURATED FAT 3.9G)
PROTEIN 22.7G CARBOHYDRATE 33.1G
CHOLESTEROL 20MG SODIUM 565MG

FYI

The flavor and intensity of dried herbs and spices deteriorate over time. For best results, purchase only small amounts of the freshest ones available. Even though old seasonings are safe to use, they will have a dull color and won't add much flavor.

Store dried seasonings in a cool, dry, dark place. Although it is convenient to keep seasonings near the cooktop or oven, the heat will speed their deterioration. To maximize the shelf life of seasonings, store them in the freezer.

Dried herbs can be used in most recipes calling for fresh ones. Because dried herbs are stronger, use only one-third the amount recommended for fresh herbs.

Shepherd's Pie (recipe on page 114)

Main-Dish Vegetables

*A*lways recognized as a storehouse of nutrition, vegetables have become the food of choice not only for vegetarians but also for those who like an occasional meatless meal. Legumes, in particular, are valued as a major source of protein, and these are enjoyed today in a wide variety of local as well as international dishes. Pinto-Tortilla Melts (page 105) hails from Mexico, while Spicy Black Beans and Rice (page 99) is a low-fat version of Cuba's favorite legume dish.

Included in this chapter are dishes featuring tofu, a soybean product that also provides an abundance of protein. Rounding out the collection of main-dish vegetable recipes is a selection of familiar vegetables paired with grains or pasta. Vegetable Kabobs with Herbed Couscous (page 117) is an eye-catching entrée and has more than 14 grams of protein per serving.

Black Bean and Corn Wontons

BLACK BEAN AND CORN WONTONS

½ cup drained canned no-salt-added black beans
2 tablespoons no-salt-added salsa
¼ cup frozen whole kernel corn, thawed
2½ tablespoons minced green onions
¼ teaspoon ground cumin
20 fresh or frozen wonton skins, thawed
½ (7-ounce) jar diced sweet red pepper, drained
½ cup nonfat cottage cheese
2½ tablespoons light beer
2 cloves garlic, minced
¼ cup (1 ounce) shredded fat-free mozzarella cheese
1 tablespoon grated Parmesan cheese
3 quarts water
Vegetable cooking spray
Fresh cilantro sprigs (optional)

Combine beans and salsa; mash with a potato masher. Stir in corn, green onions, and cumin.

Place bean mixture in centers of 10 wonton skins. Brush edges of wontons with water; top with remaining 10 wontons. Press edges together to seal, pushing out air. Trim edges with a fluted pastry wheel. Cover with a damp towel until ready to cook.

Combine red pepper and next 3 ingredients in container of an electric blender; cover and process until smooth. Transfer pepper mixture to a saucepan; add cheeses. Cook, stirring constantly, until cheeses melt. Remove from heat, and keep warm.

Bring 3 quarts water to a boil in a Dutch oven. Add filled wontons; return water to a boil. Reduce heat; simmer 4 to 5 minutes or until tender. Remove wontons with a slotted spoon; drain well.

Place wontons on a baking sheet coated with cooking spray. Broil 5½ inches from heat (with electric oven door partially opened) 3 to 4 minutes.

Spoon pepper mixture evenly onto 2 serving plates. Place 5 wontons on each plate. Garnish with cilantro sprigs, if desired. Yield: 2 servings.

PER SERVING: 423 CALORIES (6% FROM FAT)
FAT 2.9G (SATURATED FAT 0.8G)
PROTEIN 28.3G   CARBOHYDRATE 71.8G
CHOLESTEROL 15MG   SODIUM 878MG

SPICY BLACK BEANS AND RICE

1 pound dried black beans
Vegetable cooking spray
2 teaspoons olive oil
1 cup chopped onion
½ cup chopped sweet red pepper
½ cup chopped green pepper
5 cloves garlic, minced
5 cups water
1 (6-ounce) can no-salt-added tomato paste
1 (4-ounce) jar diced pimiento, undrained
2 tablespoons seeded, minced jalapeño pepper
1 tablespoon vinegar
1 teaspoon ground cumin
1 teaspoon hot sauce
¾ teaspoon salt
¼ teaspoon pepper
4½ cups cooked long-grain rice (cooked without salt or fat)

Sort and wash beans; place in a Dutch oven. Cover with water to a depth of 2 inches above beans; let soak 8 hours. Drain and rinse beans. Return beans to pan, and set aside.

Coat a large nonstick skillet with cooking spray; add oil. Place skillet over medium-high heat until hot. Add onion, sweet red pepper, green pepper, and garlic; sauté 4 to 5 minutes or until tender.

Add onion mixture, 5 cups water, and next 8 ingredients to beans; bring to a boil. Cover, reduce heat, and simmer 2 hours or until beans are tender, stirring occasionally.

To serve, place ½ cup cooked rice in each individual serving bowl; spoon 1 cup bean mixture over each serving. Yield: 9 servings.

PER SERVING: 342 CALORIES (6% FROM FAT)
FAT 2.3G (SATURATED FAT 0.4G)
PROTEIN 14.9G   CARBOHYDRATE 67.1G
CHOLESTEROL 0MG   SODIUM 216MG

BLACK AND WHITE BEANS WITH ORZO

(pictured on page 2)

Vegetable cooking spray
2 teaspoons olive oil
¾ cup chopped onion
2 teaspoons minced garlic
1 (15-ounce) can black beans, drained
1 (16-ounce) can navy beans, drained
1½ cups canned vegetable broth, undiluted
    and divided
2 cups water, divided
½ teaspoon ground cumin
1 cup orzo, uncooked
2 teaspoons curry powder
¼ teaspoon ground red pepper
1 cup diced zucchini
1 cup cauliflower flowerets
1 cup diced fresh green beans
¾ cup seeded, chopped plum tomato

Coat a large heavy skillet with cooking spray; place over medium-high heat until hot. Add olive oil, onion, and garlic; sauté 3 to 5 minutes or until onion is tender. Stir in black and navy beans, ½ cup vegetable broth, ½ cup water, and cumin. Bring to a boil; reduce heat, and simmer, uncovered, 10 to 15 minutes or until liquid is absorbed, stirring frequently. Set aside, and keep warm.

Place remaining 1 cup vegetable broth and remaining 1½ cups water in a medium saucepan; bring to a boil. Add orzo, curry powder, and red pepper. Cover, reduce heat, and simmer 25 to 30 minutes or until liquid is absorbed and orzo is tender, stirring occasionally. Set aside; keep warm.

Arrange zucchini, cauliflower, and green beans in a vegetable steamer over boiling water. Cover and steam 2 to 3 minutes or until crisp-tender. Combine orzo mixture and steamed vegetables; toss gently. Spoon orzo mixture onto a platter; top with bean mixture, and sprinkle with tomato. Yield: 6 servings.

PER SERVING: 294 CALORIES (10% FROM FAT)
FAT 3.2G (SATURATED FAT 0.5G)
PROTEIN 13.8G   CARBOHYDRATE 54.1G
CHOLESTEROL 0MG   SODIUM 473MG

BEAN-GOAT CHEESE TOSTADAS

Vegetable cooking spray
1 teaspoon olive oil
1 cup chopped purple onion
1 teaspoon chili powder
½ teaspoon ground cumin
2 (15-ounce) cans cannellini beans, drained
1 (4-ounce) can chopped green chiles, drained
2 tablespoons lime juice
8 (6-inch) corn tortillas
Bibb lettuce leaves
3½ cups shredded arugula
½ cup chopped fresh cilantro
5 ounces goat cheese, crumbled
½ cup nonfat sour cream
Tomato-Mango Salsa

Coat a saucepan with cooking spray; add oil. Place over medium-high heat until hot. Add onion, chili powder, and cumin; sauté 3 minutes or until tender. Add beans, chiles, and lime juice; stir well. Reduce heat to low; cook until heated, mashing beans with a potato masher. Set aside; keep warm.

Place tortillas on a baking sheet coated with cooking spray. Bake at 350° for 6 minutes; turn and bake an additional 6 minutes or until crisp.

Place 1 tortilla on each serving plate; top each with equal amounts of Bibb lettuce leaves, arugula, cilantro, bean mixture, cheese, and sour cream. Serve with Tomato-Mango Salsa. Yield: 8 servings.

TOMATO-MANGO SALSA
¾ cup seeded, diced tomato
½ cup peeled, diced ripe mango
¼ cup diced purple onion
¼ cup chopped fresh cilantro
2 tablespoons lime juice
1½ teaspoons seeded, minced jalapeño pepper

Combine all ingredients in a small bowl; stir well. Cover and chill at least 2 hours. Yield: 1½ cups.

PER SERVING: 234 CALORIES (23% FROM FAT)
FAT 5.9G (SATURATED FAT 2.9G)
PROTEIN 12.3G   CARBOHYDRATE 34.6G
CHOLESTEROL 16MG   SODIUM 407MG

Bean-Goat Cheese Tostadas

Pastry-Wrapped Chiles Rellenos

PASTRY-WRAPPED CHILES RELLENOS

1 cup drained canned cannellini beans,
     mashed
½ cup frozen whole kernel corn, thawed
¼ cup (1 ounce) shredded reduced-fat
     Monterey Jack cheese
2½ tablespoons minced purple onion
½ teaspoon dried basil
½ teaspoon dried oregano
4 (4-ounce) cans whole green chiles
1 (16-ounce) package commercial frozen
     phyllo pastry, thawed
Vegetable cooking spray
1¼ cups no-salt-added salsa
½ cup plus 2 tablespoons nonfat sour cream
Sliced green onions (optional)

Combine first 6 ingredients; stir well.

Drain chiles. Set 10 chiles aside; reserve remaining chiles for another use. Make a lengthwise slit down each chile. Carefully stuff bean mixture evenly into chiles; gently reshape chiles.

Place 1 sheet of phyllo on a damp towel (keep remaining phyllo covered). Lightly coat phyllo with cooking spray. Top with 1 sheet phyllo; lightly coat with cooking spray. Fold phyllo in half crosswise, bringing short ends together. Lightly coat with cooking spray.

Place 1 stuffed chile in center of phyllo, parallel with short edge and 1½ inches from bottom edge. Fold sides over chile. Roll up phyllo, jellyroll fashion, starting with short side. Place, seam side down, on an ungreased baking sheet. Lightly coat phyllo with cooking spray. Repeat procedure with remaining phyllo and stuffed chiles.

Bake at 400° for 16 minutes or until crisp and golden. Place 2 chiles rellenos on each serving plate; top each serving with ¼ cup salsa and 2 tablespoons sour cream. Garnish with green onions, if desired. Yield: 5 servings.

PER SERVING: 401 CALORIES (19% FROM FAT)
FAT 8.5G (SATURATED FAT 1.8G)
PROTEIN 13.9G   CARBOHYDRATE 65.9G
CHOLESTEROL 4MG   SODIUM 659MG

BLACK BEAN ENCHILADAS

2 (15-ounce) cans black beans, rinsed and
    drained
Vegetable cooking spray
1¼ cups finely chopped onion
2 cloves garlic, minced
1 tablespoon lime juice
½ teaspoon dried oregano
¼ teaspoon salt
½ cup nonfat sour cream
1 tablespoon plus 1 teaspoon minced fresh
    cilantro
8 (6-inch) corn tortillas
Enchilada Sauce
1 cup (4 ounces) shredded reduced-fat
    Monterey Jack cheese

Mash half of beans; set mashed and unmashed beans aside.

Coat a nonstick skillet with cooking spray; place over medium-high heat until hot. Add onion and garlic; sauté until tender. Stir in mashed and unmashed beans, lime juice, oregano, and salt; set aside.

Combine sour cream and cilantro; stir well, and set aside.

Wrap tortillas in aluminum foil; bake at 325° for 12 minutes or until thoroughly heated. Spread 1 tablespoon sour cream mixture over surface of each tortilla. Spoon bean mixture evenly down center of each tortilla. Loosely roll up tortillas.

Spread ¾ cup Enchilada Sauce in an 11- x 7- x 1½-inch baking dish coated with cooking spray. Arrange tortillas, seam side down, over sauce. Top tortillas with remaining Enchilada Sauce. Cover and bake at 350° for 15 minutes. Sprinkle evenly with cheese. Bake, uncovered, an additional 5 minutes or until cheese melts. Yield: 8 servings.

ENCHILADA SAUCE
Vegetable cooking spray
1½ tablespoons reduced-calorie margarine
2 cloves garlic, minced
2 tablespoons all-purpose flour
2 cups water
½ cup no-salt-added tomato sauce
1 tablespoon chili powder
1 tablespoon hot chili powder
¼ teaspoon salt
⅛ teaspoon dried oregano
⅛ teaspoon ground cumin

Coat a medium saucepan with cooking spray; add margarine. Place over medium heat until margarine melts. Add minced garlic; sauté until tender. Add flour, stirring until smooth. Cook 1 minute, stirring constantly.

Combine water and next 6 ingredients; add to flour mixture, stirring constantly. Bring to a boil; reduce heat, and simmer 15 minutes, stirring occasionally. Yield: 2 cups.

PER SERVING: 238 CALORIES (23% FROM FAT)
FAT 6.1G (SATURATED FAT 2.1G)
PROTEIN 13.5G   CARBOHYDRATE 34.3G
CHOLESTEROL 9MG   SODIUM 507MG

Curried Garbanzo Beans and Potatoes

CURRIED GARBANZO BEANS AND POTATOES

2 teaspoons vegetable oil
1 cup diced sweet yellow pepper
½ cup finely chopped onion
1 tablespoon plus 1 teaspoon all-purpose flour
1 teaspoon curry powder
½ teaspoon salt
½ teaspoon ground cumin
¼ to ½ teaspoon pepper
2½ cups water
1¾ cups diced unpeeled round red potato
    (about 10 ounces)
1 cup peeled, sliced Granny Smith apple
1 cup frozen English peas, thawed
1 (15-ounce) can garbanzo beans, drained
6 cups cooked long-grain rice (cooked without
    salt or fat)

Heat oil in a large nonstick skillet over medium heat. Add yellow pepper and onion; sauté 6 minutes or until tender.

Sprinkle with flour and next 4 ingredients. Stir well, and cook for an additional 30 seconds.

Add 2½ cups water and potato; reduce heat, cover, and simmer 25 minutes or until potato is tender. Add apple, peas, and beans; cover and cook an additional 10 minutes. For each serving, spoon 1 cup bean mixture over 1 cup rice. Yield: 6 servings.

PER SERVING: 398 CALORIES (7% FROM FAT)
FAT 3.2G (SATURATED FAT 0.5G)
PROTEIN 11.2G   CARBOHYDRATE 80.5G
CHOLESTEROL 0MG   SODIUM 323MG

PINTO-TORTILLA MELTS

1½ cups chopped tomato
⅓ cup chopped onion
1 (4-ounce) can chopped green chiles,
    undrained
1 clove garlic, minced
¼ teaspoon salt
1 (15-ounce) can pinto beans, drained
½ teaspoon chili powder
¼ teaspoon ground cumin
⅛ teaspoon ground red pepper
6 (6-inch) corn tortillas
¼ cup minced fresh cilantro
2 (4-ounce) cans chopped green chiles,
    undrained
¾ cup (3 ounces) shredded reduced-fat sharp
    Cheddar cheese

Combine first 5 ingredients in a saucepan. Bring to a boil over medium heat; reduce heat, and simmer, uncovered, 25 minutes, stirring occasionally. Transfer mixture to a bowl; cover and chill.

Mash beans with a potato masher. Combine beans and next 3 ingredients; stir well. Spread 2½ tablespoons bean mixture over surface of each tortilla. Top each evenly with cilantro, green chiles, and cheese.

Place tortillas on a baking sheet. Bake at 450° for 3 to 5 minutes or until cheese melts. Serve with chile sauce. Yield: 6 servings.

PER SERVING: 178 CALORIES (19% FROM FAT)
FAT 3.7G (SATURATED FAT 1.7G)
PROTEIN 10.1G   CARBOHYDRATE 28.1G
CHOLESTEROL 9MG   SODIUM 582MG

FYI

Legumes are available fresh, canned, frozen, and dried. Before cooking dried legumes, always rinse and sort them to remove any debris that may have been missed in the initial cleaning.

Dried legumes must be soaked 6 to 8 hours before cooking (lentils are an exception). For a quicker cooking method, cover legumes with cold water to 2 inches above legumes, removing any that float to the top. Bring to a rolling boil over medium-high heat, and cook 2 minutes. Remove from heat; cover and let stand 1 hour. Drain beans, and cook as directed.

Sweet-and-Tangy Lentils and Rice

SWEET-AND-TANGY LENTILS AND RICE

1 (7-ounce) jar roasted red peppers in water
⅓ cup minced fresh cilantro
3 tablespoons chopped ripe olives
2 teaspoons lemon juice
½ teaspoon curry powder
2 cloves garlic, crushed
3 cups water
1¾ cups dried lentils
¾ cup sliced green onions
⅓ cup mango chutney
3 tablespoons honey
2 teaspoons dry mustard
3 cups cooked instant rice (cooked without salt or fat)
Fresh cilantro sprigs (optional)

Drain peppers, reserving liquid. Chop 3 peppers; reserve remaining peppers in liquid for another use. Combine chopped pepper, minced cilantro, and next 4 ingredients in a small bowl. Cover and set aside.

Combine water, lentils, and green onions in a saucepan; bring to a boil. Cover, reduce heat, and simmer 10 minutes. Stir in chutney, honey, and mustard; simmer, uncovered, 20 minutes or until lentils are tender.

Place ½ cup cooked rice on each individual serving plate; top evenly with lentil mixture. Spoon pepper mixture evenly over lentil mixture. Garnish with cilantro sprigs, if desired. Yield: 6 servings.

PER SERVING: 398 CALORIES (4% FROM FAT)
FAT 1.7G (SATURATED FAT 0.2G)
PROTEIN 18.7G   CARBOHYDRATE 78.5G
CHOLESTEROL 0MG   SODIUM 219MG

CURRIED SPLIT PEAS WITH RICE

1⅔ cups dried yellow split peas
5 cups water
Vegetable cooking spray
1½ tablespoons reduced-calorie margarine
3 cups chopped onion
1 tablespoon grated unsweetened coconut
1 teaspoon crushed red pepper flakes
2 teaspoons peeled, grated gingerroot
½ teaspoon ground bay leaves
2 tablespoons all-purpose flour
1 tablespoon curry powder
1 cup skim milk
½ cup canned vegetable or chicken broth, undiluted
1 teaspoon lemon juice
¼ teaspoon salt
4½ cups cooked long-grain rice (cooked without salt or fat)
¼ cup sliced green onions
¼ cup raisins

Combine peas and water in a Dutch oven. Bring to a boil; cover, reduce heat, and simmer 40 to 45 minutes or until peas are tender. Drain well, and set aside.

Coat a large nonstick skillet with cooking spray; add margarine. Place over medium heat until margarine melts. Add onion and next 4 ingredients; sauté 3 to 4 minutes or until onion is tender. Add flour and curry powder, stirring well. Cook 1 minute, stirring constantly. Gradually add milk and vegetable broth to flour mixture. Cook over medium heat, stirring constantly, until mixture is thickened and bubbly.

Remove from heat; stir in peas, lemon juice, and salt. Cook until mixture is thoroughly heated, stirring occasionally. For each serving, top ¾ cup rice with 1 cup pea mixture. Top each serving with 2 teaspoons green onions and 2 teaspoons raisins. Yield: 6 servings.

PER SERVING: 447 CALORIES (8% FROM FAT)
FAT 4.0G (SATURATED FAT 1.6G)
PROTEIN 19.3G   CARBOHYDRATE 85.5G
CHOLESTEROL 1MG   SODIUM 313MG

Bean and Tofu Jambalaya

Tofu, or soybean curd, is available in various degrees of firmness, depending on how much whey, or liquid, has been pressed out during processing.

Vegetable cooking spray
½ cup chopped onion
½ cup chopped green pepper
1 clove garlic, minced
2 (14½-ounce) cans no-salt-added whole tomatoes, undrained and chopped
1 (15-ounce) can pinto beans, drained
1 (15.8-ounce) can Great Northern beans, drained
¼ cup low-sodium Worcestershire sauce
1 tablespoon vinegar
1 teaspoon chili powder
½ teaspoon salt
½ teaspoon dried thyme
½ teaspoon rubbed sage
½ teaspoon ground red pepper
½ teaspoon freshly ground black pepper
¼ teaspoon garlic powder
⅔ cup long-grain rice, uncooked
6 ounces firm tofu, drained and cut into ½-inch cubes

Coat a large saucepan with cooking spray; place over medium-high heat until hot. Add onion, green pepper, and garlic; sauté until tender. Add tomatoes and next 11 ingredients; stir well. Bring mixture to a boil; stir in rice. Cover, reduce heat, and simmer 20 minutes. Add tofu, stirring gently; cover and cook an additional 5 minutes or until rice is tender. Yield: 6 servings.

Per Serving: 237 Calories (9% from Fat)
Fat 2.3g (Saturated Fat 0.3g)
Protein 11.1g Carbohydrate 44.8g
Cholesterol 0mg Sodium 460mg

Tofu-Zucchini Stroganoff

1 (10½-ounce) package firm tofu
Vegetable cooking spray
1 teaspoon vegetable oil
1 medium zucchini, cut into thin strips
1 medium-size sweet red pepper, cut into thin strips
½ pound fresh mushrooms, sliced
2 cloves garlic, minced
⅔ cup skim milk
1 tablespoon all-purpose flour
½ teaspoon salt
½ teaspoon dried dillweed
1 tablespoon Neufchâtel cheese, softened
4 cups cooked medium egg noodles (cooked without salt or fat)

Wrap tofu in several layers of cheesecloth or paper towels; press lightly to remove excess moisture. Remove cheesecloth; cut tofu into ½-inch cubes.

Coat a large nonstick skillet with cooking spray; add oil. Place over medium-high heat until hot. Add tofu; sauté 3 to 4 minutes or until lightly browned. Drain tofu; pat dry with paper towels. Wipe skillet with a paper towel.

Coat skillet with cooking spray, and place over medium-high heat until hot. Add zucchini and next 3 ingredients; sauté until tender. Remove vegetable mixture from skillet, and set aside. Wipe skillet dry with a paper towel.

Combine milk, flour, salt, and dillweed in a small bowl, stirring well. Add flour mixture to skillet; bring to a boil over medium heat, stirring constantly. Add cheese; cook, stirring constantly, until cheese melts. Add tofu and vegetable mixture. Cook over low heat, stirring constantly, until thoroughly heated. To serve, spoon tofu mixture evenly over noodles. Yield: 4 servings.

Per Serving: 342 Calories (23% from Fat)
Fat 8.6g (Saturated Fat 1.9g)
Protein 17.6g Carbohydrate 50.8g
Cholesterol 56mg Sodium 350mg

SPICY CHILI MAC

Vegetable cooking spray
1½ cups finely chopped onion
1⅓ cups finely chopped green pepper
2 cloves garlic, minced
1 tablespoon chili powder
1 teaspoon ground cumin
½ teaspoon garlic powder
½ teaspoon dried crushed red pepper
1 (28-ounce) can crushed tomatoes with puree, undrained
½ pound firm tofu, drained and crumbled
2 (15-ounce) cans red kidney beans, drained
7 ounces wagon wheel pasta, uncooked
¼ cup plus 3 tablespoons (1¾ ounces) shredded reduced-fat Cheddar cheese

Coat a Dutch oven with cooking spray, and place over medium-high heat until hot. Add chopped onion, chopped green pepper, and minced garlic, and sauté vegetable mixture until tender.

Add chili powder, cumin, garlic powder, and crushed red pepper; sauté 1 minute, stirring constantly. Stir in tomatoes and tofu. Bring mixture to a boil; reduce heat, and simmer, uncovered, 15 minutes. Add kidney beans, and cook an additional 10 minutes or until bean mixture is thoroughly heated.

Cook pasta according to package directions, omitting salt and fat; drain.

To serve, place ½ cup pasta in each of 7 individual serving bowls, and spoon 1 cup chili over pasta. Top each serving with 1 tablespoon cheese. Yield: 7 servings.

PER SERVING: 291 CALORIES (13% FROM FAT)
FAT 4.3G (SATURATED FAT 1.2G)
PROTEIN 16.5G   CARBOHYDRATE 48.5G
CHOLESTEROL 5MG   SODIUM 354MG

Spicy Chili Mac

Corn and Tomato Frittata

CORN AND TOMATO FRITTATA

This frittata is an easy supper or brunch entrée. Expect it to serve only four if the appetites are hearty.

Vegetable cooking spray
1¼ cups fresh corn cut from cob (about 3 ears)
¼ cup chopped green onions
1½ cups frozen egg substitute, thawed
⅓ cup skim milk
1½ teaspoons minced fresh basil
⅛ teaspoon salt
⅛ teaspoon pepper
2 small tomatoes, cut into 12 wedges
1 cup (4 ounces) shredded reduced-fat Cheddar cheese
Fresh basil sprigs (optional)

Coat a medium nonstick skillet with cooking spray; place over medium-high heat until hot. Add corn and green onions; sauté until tender. Combine egg substitute and next 4 ingredients; stir well.

Pour egg mixture over vegetables in skillet. Cover and cook over medium-low heat 15 minutes or until mixture is almost set.

Arrange tomato wedges near center of egg mixture, and sprinkle with Cheddar cheese. Cover and cook an additional 5 minutes or until cheese melts. Cut frittata into 6 wedges. Garnish with fresh basil sprigs, if desired, and serve immediately. Yield: 6 servings.

PER SERVING: 133 CALORIES (29% FROM FAT)
FAT 4.3G (SATURATED FAT 2.2G)
PROTEIN 13.7G   CARBOHYDRATE 11.2G
CHOLESTEROL 12MG   SODIUM 295MG

EGGPLANT ROLL-UPS

Nonfat cottage cheese works best in this recipe because it has a drier texture than low-fat cottage cheese, which is creamier and would make the filling too thin.

2 tablespoons all-purpose flour
1 tablespoon chili powder
¼ teaspoon salt
¼ teaspoon ground oregano
Dash of ground cumin
1½ cups water
½ cup no-salt-added tomato sauce
1 (1½-pound) eggplant
½ cup nonfat cottage cheese
½ cup (2 ounces) shredded reduced-fat Monterey Jack cheese
3 tablespoons minced green onions, divided
1 jalapeño pepper, seeded and minced

Combine first 5 ingredients in a medium saucepan, stirring well. Gradually stir in water and tomato sauce. Bring to a boil over medium heat, stirring constantly. Reduce heat, and simmer, uncovered, 15 minutes, stirring frequently. Set tomato sauce mixture aside, and keep warm.

Peel eggplant, and cut lengthwise into 8 (¼-inch-thick) slices. Place eggplant slices in a Dutch oven. Add water to cover. Bring to a boil, and cook 2 to 3 minutes or until eggplant is tender. Press dry between paper towels.

Combine cottage cheese, Monterey Jack cheese, 2 tablespoons onions, and jalapeño pepper. Spoon about 2 tablespoons cheese mixture down center of each eggplant slice; roll up jellyroll fashion.

Spread ½ cup tomato sauce mixture over bottom of an 11- x 7- x 1½-inch baking dish. Place eggplant rolls, seam side down, over sauce. Spoon remaining sauce over rolls. Sprinkle with remaining 1 tablespoon green onions. Bake, uncovered, at 400° for 20 minutes or until thoroughly heated. Yield: 4 servings.

PER SERVING: 130 CALORIES (22% FROM FAT)
FAT 3.2G (SATURATED FAT 1.7G)
PROTEIN 10.6G   CARBOHYDRATE 17.2G
CHOLESTEROL 11MG   SODIUM 374MG

ITALIAN STUFFED EGGPLANT

2 medium eggplants
Vegetable cooking spray
1¼ cups chopped onion
1¼ cups diced zucchini
1 cup sliced fresh mushrooms
¾ cup chopped green pepper
1 clove garlic, minced
¾ cup chopped tomato
1 (8-ounce) can no-salt-added tomato sauce
1 cup cooked brown rice (cooked without salt or fat)
¼ cup grated Parmesan cheese
1 tablespoon unsalted sunflower kernels, toasted
1 teaspoon dried Italian seasoning
1 cup (4 ounces) shredded part-skim mozzarella cheese

Wash eggplants; cut each in half lengthwise. Carefully remove pulp, leaving a ¼-inch-thick shell. Chop pulp, reserving 2 cups. (Reserve remaining pulp for other uses.) Set eggplant shells aside.

Coat a nonstick skillet with cooking spray; place over medium heat until hot. Add onion and next 4 ingredients; sauté until tender. Stir in 2 cups reserved eggplant, tomato, and tomato sauce. Cook, uncovered, 15 minutes, stirring occasionally. Remove from heat; stir in rice, Parmesan cheese, sunflower kernels, and Italian seasoning.

Place eggplant shells in a shallow baking dish coated with cooking spray. Spoon vegetable mixture evenly into shells. Bake, uncovered, at 350° for 10 minutes or until thoroughly heated. Sprinkle with cheese; bake an additional 5 minutes or until cheese melts. Yield 4 servings.

PER SERVING: 295 CALORIES (28% FROM FAT)
FAT 9.2G (SATURATED FAT 4.2G)
PROTEIN 16.1G   CARBOHYDRATE 41.4G
CHOLESTEROL 20MG   SODIUM 258MG

KALE AND SPINACH BAKE

2 teaspoons olive oil
1 cup finely chopped onion
2 cloves garlic, minced
9¾ cups tightly packed chopped fresh kale (about 1 pound)
6⅓ cups tightly packed chopped fresh spinach (about 1 pound)
Vegetable cooking spray
¾ cup plain low-fat yogurt
¼ cup grated Parmesan cheese
2½ tablespoons all-purpose flour
⅛ teaspoon salt
⅛ teaspoon ground nutmeg
⅛ teaspoon pepper
1 (16-ounce) carton 1% low-fat cottage cheese
2 eggs
1 egg white
1½ tablespoons grated Parmesan cheese

Heat oil in a Dutch oven over medium heat. Add onion and garlic; sauté 3 minutes. Add kale and spinach, stirring well. Reduce heat to medium-low; cover and cook 20 minutes or until wilted, stirring occasionally. Remove from heat, and spoon into a 2-quart baking dish coated with cooking spray. Set aside.

Position knife blade in food processor bowl; add yogurt and next 8 ingredients. Process until smooth. Pour yogurt mixture over greens, stirring gently. Sprinkle with 1½ tablespoons Parmesan cheese. Bake, uncovered, at 350° for 40 minutes. Yield: 6 (1-cup) servings.

PER SERVING: 226 CALORIES (27% FROM FAT)
FAT 6.9G (SATURATED FAT 2.5G)
PROTEIN 21.4G   CARBOHYDRATE 22.7G
CHOLESTEROL 79MG   SODIUM 586MG

Cheese-Stuffed Potatoes

CHEESE-STUFFED POTATOES

6 medium baking potatoes (about 2½ pounds)
¾ cup plus 2 tablespoons (3½ ounces)
   shredded reduced-fat sharp Cheddar cheese
1½ cups nonfat sour cream
⅓ cup finely chopped green onions
¼ teaspoon salt
Paprika

Bake potatoes at 400° for 1 hour or until done; let cool slightly. Cut a ¼-inch-thick slice from the top of each baked potato; carefully scoop pulp into a bowl, leaving shells intact. Add cheese and sour cream to pulp, and mash; stir in chopped green onions and salt.

Stuff shells with potato mixture, and sprinkle with paprika. Place on a baking sheet, and bake at 450° for 15 minutes or until thoroughly heated. Yield: 6 servings.

Note: Potatoes may be cooked in the microwave oven. Pierce potatoes with a fork, and arrange in a circle on paper towels in microwave oven. Microwave at HIGH 16 minutes or until done, turning and rearranging potatoes halfway through cooking time. Let stand 5 minutes. Scoop out pulp; mash pulp, and season. Stuff potato shells with potato mixture. Sprinkle with paprika. Microwave at HIGH 5 minutes or until thoroughly heated.

PER SERVING: 280 CALORIES (11% FROM FAT)
FAT 3.3G (SATURATED FAT 1.9G)
PROTEIN 12.7G   CARBOHYDRATE 48.7G
CHOLESTEROL 11MG   SODIUM 272MG

SHEPHERD'S PIE
(pictured on page 96)

3 cups frozen peas and carrots, thawed
1 cup frozen chopped onion, thawed
1 cup frozen chopped green pepper, thawed
2 teaspoons dried thyme
2 teaspoons sweet Hungarian paprika
Olive oil-flavored vegetable cooking spray
4 cups frozen hash browns, thawed
⅔ cup light ricotta cheese
¼ teaspoon salt
2 cups drained canned black-eyed peas
1 cup diced tomato
1 (8-ounce) can no-salt-added tomato sauce
2 teaspoons low-sodium Worcestershire sauce
¼ teaspoon salt
Sweet Hungarian paprika

Combine first 5 ingredients; stir well. Spoon into a 15- x 10- x 1-inch jellyroll pan coated with cooking spray; coat vegetables with cooking spray. Bake, uncovered, at 400° for 20 minutes, stirring after 10 minutes; set aside.

Cook hash browns in boiling water to cover 10 minutes or until tender. Drain and mash. Stir in ricotta cheese and salt; set aside.

Combine vegetable mixture, black-eyed peas, and next 4 ingredients, stirring well. Spoon into a 2½-quart shallow baking dish coated with cooking spray.

Spoon hash brown mixture in a border around edge of dish; spoon remaining hash brown mixture over center of dish. Sprinkle additional paprika over top. Bake, uncovered, at 350° for 20 minutes. Yield: 6 servings.

PER SERVING: 215 CALORIES (8% FROM FAT)
FAT 1.9G (SATURATED FAT 0.7G)
PROTEIN 11.4G   CARBOHYDRATE 40.2G
CHOLESTEROL 4MG   SODIUM 455MG

MEXICAN POTATO RAGOÛT

1 pound round red potatoes, quartered
1 tablespoon olive oil, divided
2 cups diced onion
3 tablespoons chopped garlic
Vegetable cooking spray
2 cups cubed eggplant
2 cups cubed zucchini
1 cup coarsely chopped green pepper
1 (15-ounce) can garbanzo beans, drained
4 plum tomatoes, cut into thin wedges
½ cup minced fresh cilantro
2 teaspoons dried oregano
1 teaspoon grated lemon rind
½ teaspoon ground cumin
¼ teaspoon salt
1½ cups (6 ounces) shredded nonfat Monterey Jack cheese

Cook potato in boiling water to cover 10 to 15 minutes or just until tender. Drain and set aside.

Heat 1 teaspoon olive oil in a large nonstick skillet over medium-high heat. Add onion and garlic; sauté 5 minutes. Transfer to a 13- x 9- x 2-inch baking dish coated with cooking spray.

Add remaining 2 teaspoons olive oil to skillet; add eggplant, zucchini, and green pepper; cook over medium heat 5 minutes, stirring frequently. Transfer to baking dish; add beans and next 6 ingredients, stirring well. Cover and bake at 350° for 30 minutes.

Stir in reserved potato; sprinkle with cheese. Bake, uncovered, an additional 15 minutes or until thoroughly heated. Yield: 6 servings.

PER SERVING: 245 CALORIES (15% FROM FAT)
FAT 4.1G (SATURATED FAT 0.5G)
PROTEIN 14.0G   CARBOHYDRATE 38.2G
CHOLESTEROL 5MG   SODIUM 401MG

HEARTY VEGETABLE PIZZA

1 cup regular oats, uncooked
1 package active dry yeast
½ cup plus 2 tablespoons warm water (105° to 115°)
1 teaspoon sugar
½ teaspoon salt
1½ tablespoons vegetable oil
½ cup whole wheat flour
¼ cup plus 2 tablespoons all-purpose flour, divided
Vegetable cooking spray
1 (10-ounce) package frozen chopped spinach
2 cups thinly sliced leeks
1 small sweet red pepper, cut into strips
1 clove garlic, minced
⅔ cup no-salt-added tomato sauce
½ teaspoon dried Italian seasoning
½ cup sliced fresh mushrooms
6 cherry tomatoes, quartered
1 cup (4 ounces) shredded part-skim mozzarella cheese

Place oats in container of an electric blender or food processor; cover and process until oats resemble flour.

Dissolve yeast in warm water in a large mixing bowl; let stand 5 minutes. Add ground oats, sugar, salt, and oil; beat at medium speed of an electric mixer until well blended. Add whole wheat flour to oats mixture; beat at medium speed of an electric mixer 1 minute. Gradually stir in ¼ cup all-purpose flour to make a soft dough.

Sprinkle 1 tablespoon all-purpose flour evenly over work surface; turn dough out onto floured surface, and knead until smooth and elastic (about 5 minutes). Place dough in a large bowl coated with cooking spray, turning to coat top. Cover and let rise in a warm place (85°), free from drafts, 1 hour or until doubled in bulk.

Cook spinach according to package directions, omitting salt; drain. Press spinach between paper towels until barely moist; set aside.

Coat a large nonstick skillet with cooking spray; place over medium-high heat until hot. Add leeks, pepper, and garlic; sauté until tender. Stir in spinach, and set aside.

Punch dough down. Sprinkle remaining 1 tablespoon all-purpose flour evenly over work surface. Turn dough out onto floured surface; roll to a 14-inch circle. Place circle on a 12-inch pizza pan coated with cooking spray. Turn excess dough under to form a rim. Prick bottom of crust with a fork. Bake at 400° for 5 minutes.

Combine tomato sauce and Italian seasoning; spread over crust. Top with spinach mixture, mushrooms, and tomatoes. Bake at 400° for 12 to 15 minutes or until crust is lightly browned. Sprinkle with cheese. Bake an additional 5 minutes or until cheese melts. To serve, cut pizza into 8 wedges. Yield: 4 servings.

PER SERVING: 383 CALORIES (29% FROM FAT)
FAT 12.3G (SATURATED FAT 4.2G)
PROTEIN 18.1G   CARBOHYDRATE 53.5G
CHOLESTEROL 16MG   SODIUM 504MG

Fiber Facts

Fiber lowers cholesterol levels, helps you lose weight, and may even prevent cancer. The catch is that you need to consume a lot of it—20 to 35 grams daily. Vegetarians can easily get that amount of fiber from unpeeled fruit, vegetables, legumes, whole grains, and seeds.

If you're building up your fiber intake, do so gradually over a six- to eight-week period. Also remember to drink 8 to 10 glasses of water daily. As you increase your fiber intake, water will help move the fiber through your system.

ZUCCHINI PARMESAN

Olive oil-flavored vegetable cooking spray
1¾ cups sliced fresh mushrooms
½ cup minced shallots
6 cups peeled, seeded, and chopped tomato
1½ cups no-salt-added tomato juice
1 (6-ounce) can no-salt-added tomato paste
2 tablespoons chopped fresh basil
2 teaspoons chopped fresh oregano
½ teaspoon fennel seeds
¼ teaspoon salt
1 bay leaf
5 large zucchini
1¼ cups (5 ounces) shredded part-skim
    mozzarella cheese
¼ cup plus 2 tablespoons grated Parmesan
    cheese

Coat a Dutch oven with cooking spray. Place
over medium-high heat until hot. Add mushrooms
and shallots; sauté until vegetables are tender.

Add chopped tomato and next 7 ingredients; stir
well. Bring to a boil; reduce heat, and simmer,
uncovered, 40 minutes, stirring occasionally. Remove and discard bay leaf. Set aside; keep warm.

Cut each zucchini lengthwise into 5 slices. Cook
zucchini slices in boiling water to cover 6 to 8 minutes or until crisp-tender; drain. Rinse with cold
water, and drain again. Press slices dry between
paper towels.

Spread 2 cups tomato mixture over bottom of a
13- x 9- x 2-inch baking dish. Place half of zucchini
slices over sauce, overlapping slices slightly.
Sprinkle half of mozzarella cheese and 2 tablespoons Parmesan cheese over zucchini. Repeat layers with 2 cups tomato mixture, remaining zucchini
slices, remaining mozzarella cheese, and 2 tablespoons Parmesan cheese. Top with remaining
tomato mixture, and sprinkle with remaining 2
tablespoons Parmesan cheese.

Bake, uncovered, at 350° for 30 minutes or until
thoroughly heated. Let stand 10 minutes before
serving. Yield: 8 servings.

PER SERVING: 156 CALORIES (28% FROM FAT)
FAT 4.9G (SATURATED FAT 2.7G)
PROTEIN 10.8G   CARBOHYDRATE 21.2G
CHOLESTEROL 13MG   SODIUM 260MG

SUMMER VEGETABLE DINNER

1 small eggplant, cut into ½-inch cubes
2 tablespoons lemon juice
2 teaspoons olive oil
½ pound small fresh mushrooms, halved
2 medium-size yellow squash, cut into
    ½-inch-thick slices
2 small zucchini, cut into ½-inch-thick slices
1 medium-size sweet red pepper, seeded and
    cut into 1-inch cubes
3 tablespoons minced fresh basil
¾ teaspoon freshly ground pepper
¼ teaspoon salt
2 medium tomatoes, cut into wedges
8 ounces firm tofu, drained and cut into
    ½-inch cubes
1½ cups (6 ounces) shredded reduced-fat
    Monterey Jack cheese
6 cups cooked brown rice (cooked without salt
    or fat)

Combine eggplant and lemon juice; toss well.
Heat oil in a Dutch oven over medium heat until
hot. Add eggplant, mushrooms, and next 6 ingredients; sauté 3 to 4 minutes or until vegetables are
crisp-tender. Cover and cook 3 minutes. Add
tomato, tofu, and cheese, stirring gently; cook,
uncovered, 2 minutes or until thoroughly heated.
Place brown rice on a serving platter. Spoon vegetable mixture over rice, and serve immediately.
Yield: 8 servings.

PER SERVING: 292 CALORIES (25% FROM FAT)
FAT 8.2G (SATURATED FAT 3.0G)
PROTEIN 14.3G   CARBOHYDRATE 42.3G
CHOLESTEROL 14MG   SODIUM 225MG

VEGETABLE KABOBS WITH HERBED COUSCOUS

Serve this recipe for dinner, and you'll be following USDA's guidelines for healthy eating. It's a dish packed with complex carbohydrates.

8 small round red potatoes
1 (1-pound) eggplant
¼ cup plus 2 tablespoons lemon juice
½ cup commercial reduced-calorie Italian
    dressing
1 tablespoon chopped fresh basil
2 cloves garlic, minced
16 medium-size fresh mushrooms
2 small zucchini, cut into 16 slices
2 small purple onions, quartered
1 small sweet red pepper, cut into 8 pieces
Vegetable cooking spray
1 cup water
1 cup canned vegetable or chicken broth,
    undiluted
1⅔ cups couscous, uncooked
¼ cup minced fresh parsley
2 tablespoons chopped fresh oregano
1 tablespoon chopped fresh thyme

Cook potatoes in boiling water to cover in a medium saucepan 15 minutes or until tender; drain and set aside.

Trim ends from eggplant. Cut eggplant in half lengthwise. Place just one half, cut side down, on a cutting board. Cut vertically into ¼-inch-thick strips. Repeat procedure with remaining eggplant half.

Combine lemon juice and next 3 ingredients in a large heavy-duty, zip-top plastic bag. Add potatoes, eggplant strips, mushrooms, and next 3 ingredients; seal bag, and shake until vegetables are well coated. Marinate in refrigerator 1 hour, turning bag occasionally.

Remove vegetables from marinade, reserving marinade. Fold eggplant strips accordion-style, and thread strips alternately with other vegetables on 8 (14-inch) skewers.

Coat grill rack with cooking spray; place on grill over medium-hot coals (350° to 400°). Place kabobs on rack; grill, covered, 10 to 12 minutes or until

vegetables are tender, turning and basting occasionally with reserved marinade. Set vegetable kabobs aside, and keep warm.

Bring water and broth to a boil in a medium saucepan. Stir in couscous and next 3 ingredients. Remove from heat; cover and let stand 5 minutes. Fluff with a fork. Remove vegetables from skewers, and serve over couscous. Yield: 4 servings.

PER SERVING: 387 CALORIES (5% FROM FAT)
FAT 2.3G (SATURATED FAT 0.3G)
PROTEIN 14.1G   CARBOHYDRATE 81.6G
CHOLESTEROL 0MG   SODIUM 627MG

Place one half of eggplant cut side down; cut vertically into ¹/₂-inch-thick strips.

Thread eggplant strips accordion-style alternately with other vegetables onto 8 metal skewers.

Vegetable-Stuffed Zucchini (recipe on page 140)

COMPLEMENTARY DISHES

*T*he recipes in this chapter are not intended to be served as entrées but rather as side dishes to round out a menu. For example, try Corn and Barley Salad (page 121) with Spicy Chili Mac (page 109). Or make Italian Green Salad (page 129) to accompany Fresh Tomato Spaghetti (page 89).

If you are a semi-vegetarian, try these dishes on the side with your occasional chicken or fish recipes. Seasoned Couscous (page 130) is well matched to grilled chicken, and Colorful Coleslaw (page 124) complements almost any broiled fish.

Add these side dishes to your meals, and you'll be serving up good taste along with a wealth of vitamins, minerals, and fiber.

Corn and Barley Salad

APPLE-WILD RICE SALAD

2 cups cooked wild rice (cooked without salt or fat)
2 cups cooked long-grain rice (cooked without salt or fat)
1 cup peeled, chopped Red Delicious apple
1 cup frozen English peas, thawed
½ cup unsweetened orange juice
3 tablespoons fresh lime juice
2 tablespoons minced fresh mint
1 tablespoon vegetable oil
1½ teaspoons grated orange rind
½ teaspoon salt
⅛ teaspoon freshly ground pepper

Combine first 4 ingredients in a bowl; toss. Combine orange juice and next 6 ingredients; stir well. Pour over rice mixture. Yield: 6 (1-cup) servings.

PER SERVING: 201 CALORIES (12% FROM FAT)
FAT 2.7G (SATURATED FAT 0.5G)
PROTEIN 5.6G   CARBOHYDRATE 39.5G
CHOLESTEROL 0MG   SODIUM 220MG

CORN AND BARLEY SALAD

2 cups water
⅔ cup pearl barley, uncooked
¼ teaspoon salt
2 cups corn cut from cob or frozen whole kernel corn, thawed
½ cup thinly sliced unpeeled cucumber
½ cup (2-inch) julienne-sliced sweet red pepper
3 tablespoons white wine vinegar
1 tablespoon water
1 tablespoon vegetable oil
¼ teaspoon salt
¼ teaspoon dried basil
⅛ teaspoon ground white pepper
Boston lettuce leaves (optional)

Bring water to a boil in a saucepan; add barley and ¼ teaspoon salt. Cover, reduce heat, and simmer 40 minutes or until liquid is absorbed; let cool.

Combine barley, corn, cucumber, and red pepper in a bowl. Combine vinegar and next 5 ingredients. Pour over barley mixture; toss. Serve on lettuce-lined plates, if desired. Yield: 4 (1-cup) servings.

PER SERVING: 204 CALORIES (21% FROM FAT)
FAT 4.7G (SATURATED FAT 0.8G)
PROTEIN 5.5G   CARBOHYDRATE 38.1G
CHOLESTEROL 0MG   SODIUM 295MG

BULGUR AND BROCCOLI SALAD

1½ cups boiling water
¾ cup bulgur (cracked wheat), uncooked
2 cups chopped fresh broccoli
½ cup finely chopped carrot
¼ cup finely chopped purple onion
3 tablespoons chopped walnuts
1 tablespoon low-sodium soy sauce
½ teaspoon sugar
½ teaspoon grated lemon rind
⅛ teaspoon freshly ground pepper
3 tablespoons fresh lemon juice
1 tablespoon water
1 teaspoon vegetable oil
1 clove garlic, crushed

Combine boiling water and bulgur in a large bowl; stir. Let stand 30 minutes or until bulgur is tender and liquid is absorbed. Fluff with a fork; set aside.

Arrange broccoli in a vegetable steamer over boiling water. Cover and steam 3 minutes or until crisp-tender. Add broccoli, carrot, and onion to bulgur mixture; stir well.

Place a nonstick skillet over medium-high heat until hot. Add walnuts; cook for 3 minutes, stirring constantly. Add soy sauce, stirring constantly until sauce is absorbed. Remove from skillet; set aside.

Combine sugar and next 6 ingredients; stir well with a whisk. Add to bulgur mixture; toss well. Top with soy walnuts. Yield: 4 (1-cup) servings.

PER SERVING: 166 CALORIES (27% FROM FAT)
FAT 5.0G (SATURATED FAT 0.5G)
PROTEIN 6.5G   CARBOHYDRATE 27.4G
CHOLESTEROL 0MG   SODIUM 143MG

SOUTHWESTERN TABBOULEH

1 cup bulgur (cracked wheat), uncooked
2 cups boiling water
3 tablespoons low-sodium soy sauce
2 tablespoons lemon juice
1 tablespoon olive oil
1 cup seeded, diced tomato
1 cup peeled, minced jicama
½ cup minced fresh cilantro
3 tablespoons minced fresh chives
2 tablespoons minced fresh mint
1 tablespoon peeled, grated gingerroot
2 teaspoons minced garlic

Combine bulgur and water in a large bowl; let stand 1 hour or until bulgur is tender and liquid is absorbed.

Combine soy sauce, lemon juice, and oil, stirring well. Add to bulgur; toss well. Add tomato and remaining ingredients; toss. Cover and chill at least 4 hours. Yield: 5 (1-cup) servings.

PER SERVING: 153 CALORIES (20% FROM FAT)
FAT 3.4G (SATURATED FAT 0.5G)
PROTEIN 4.7G   CARBOHYDRATE 27.8G
CHOLESTEROL 0MG   SODIUM 254MG

Did You Know?

Lentils have been part of man's diet for centuries. Each cup of dried lentils produces about 3 cups of cooked lentils that can be refrigerated for up to four days or frozen for up to three months.

Lentils are rich in protein and carbohydrates. And unlike most legumes, they do not need to be presoaked. Lentils will cook in less than 40 minutes.

Cooked lentils have a nutty, peppery flavor. They can replace potatoes, rice, or pasta in stews, or they can stand on their own in make-ahead salads, such as the variation of tabbouleh on this page.

TABBOULEH-LENTIL SALAD

4 cups water
1 cup dried lentils
¾ cup finely chopped onion
¾ cup bulgur (cracked wheat), uncooked
¼ cup plus 2 tablespoons lemon juice
¼ cup plus 2 tablespoons canned vegetable or
  chicken broth, undiluted
1 tablespoon olive oil
⅛ teaspoon salt
¼ teaspoon freshly ground pepper
2 cloves garlic, minced
¾ cup chopped fresh parsley
¼ cup plus 2 tablespoons chopped fresh mint
2 cups seeded, diced unpeeled tomato (about 3
  medium)
Leaf lettuce leaves
¾ cup plus 2 tablespoons plain nonfat yogurt

Combine first 3 ingredients in a large saucepan; bring to a boil. Cover, reduce heat, and simmer 10 minutes. Stir in bulgur; cover and simmer 15 minutes or until lentils are tender. Drain well; spoon into a large bowl.

Combine lemon juice and next 5 ingredients; stir with a wire whisk. Add to lentil mixture; toss well. Cover and let stand at room temperature 1 hour, stirring occasionally. Stir in parsley and mint. Cover and chill 2 hours. Stir in tomato. Serve on lettuce-lined plates; top with yogurt. Yield: 7 servings.

PER SERVING: 206 CALORIES (12% FROM FAT)
FAT 2.8G (SATURATED FAT 0.4G)
PROTEIN 12.3G   CARBOHYDRATE 35.6G
CHOLESTEROL 1MG   SODIUM 134MG

Tabbouleh-Lentil Salad

QUINOA-VEGETABLE SALAD RING

1 cup quinoa, uncooked
Vegetable cooking spray
1 tablespoon olive oil
½ cup chopped onion
½ cup chopped green pepper
1 clove garlic, minced
1 cup thinly sliced zucchini
1 cup chopped yellow squash
1 cup seeded, chopped, unpeeled tomato
½ cup chopped celery
½ cup minced fresh parsley
1 tablespoon minced fresh marjoram
½ teaspoon freshly ground pepper
¼ teaspoon salt
2 tablespoons lemon juice
2 tablespoons white wine vinegar

Place quinoa in a large, fine metal strainer; rinse with cold running water, and drain. Cook according to package directions; set aside.

Coat a large skillet with cooking spray; add olive oil, and place over medium heat until hot. Add onion, green pepper, and garlic; sauté until tender. Add zucchini, yellow squash, and tomato; cook 3 minutes, stirring frequently. Remove from heat; add quinoa, celery, and remaining ingredients, tossing gently.

Lightly pack mixture into a 6-cup ring mold coated with cooking spray. Cover and chill 8 hours.

Unmold salad ring onto a serving platter; serve chilled or at room temperature. Yield: 10 (½-cup) servings.

PER SERVING: 95 CALORIES (26% FROM FAT)
FAT 2.7G (SATURATED FAT 0.3G)
PROTEIN 3.0G   CARBOHYDRATE 15.6G
CHOLESTEROL 0MG   SODIUM 79MG

COLORFUL COLESLAW

1 small head cabbage, shredded (about 2 pounds)
1½ cups frozen whole kernel corn, thawed
1 cup chopped red onion
1 cup shredded carrot
1 cup chopped sweet red pepper
½ cup sugar
½ cup white vinegar
2½ tablespoons vegetable oil
2 tablespoons water
1 teaspoon salt
1 teaspoon celery seeds
¼ teaspoon ground white pepper
¼ teaspoon mustard seeds
Dash of hot sauce

Combine first 5 ingredients in a large bowl; toss well, and set aside.

Combine sugar and next 8 ingredients in a saucepan. Bring to a boil, stirring frequently until sugar completely dissolves. Pour dressing over cabbage mixture, and toss gently until all ingredients are coated. Cover and chill at least 2 hours.

Toss gently, and serve with a slotted spoon. Yield: 12 servings.

PER SERVING: 105 CALORIES (28% FROM FAT)
FAT 3.3G (SATURATED FAT 0.4G)
PROTEIN 1.8G   CARBOHYDRATE 19.3G
CHOLESTEROL 0MG   SODIUM 211MG

Food Facts

Quinoa is an ancient South American grain that has a distinctly sweet, nutty flavor and light, fluffy texture. When cooked, the tiny, pale, seed-shaped grains become translucent and quadruple in size. Quinoa, a high-protein grain, may be eaten as a hot cereal or used interchangeably with rice in soups, casseroles, and pilafs. Look for quinoa in health-food stores and in large supermarkets.

Colorful Coleslaw

Mandarin Green Salad

4 cups tightly packed torn romaine lettuce
4 cups tightly packed torn Boston lettuce
½ cup thinly sliced red onion, separated into rings
2 (11-ounce) cans mandarin oranges in light syrup, drained
1 cup cider vinegar
½ cup sugar
2 tablespoons minced red onion
2 tablespoons vegetable oil
½ teaspoon poppy seeds

Combine first 4 ingredients in a large bowl, and set salad aside.

Combine vinegar and next 4 ingredients in container of an electric blender; cover and process until smooth. Pour ½ cup dressing over salad; toss well. Store the remaining dressing in an airtight container in the refrigerator. Yield: 5 (2-cup) servings.

PER SERVING: 94 CALORIES (21% FROM FAT)
FAT 2.2G (SATURATED FAT 0.4G)
PROTEIN 1.8G   CARBOHYDRATE 18.9G
CHOLESTEROL 0MG   SODIUM 7MG

Radicchio and Pear Salad

½ cup plain low-fat yogurt
¼ teaspoon poppy seeds
2 teaspoons lemon juice
2 teaspoons honey
2 large firm, unpeeled ripe Bartlett or Comice pears
8 large radicchio leaves
¼ cup crumbled Roquefort cheese or other blue cheese
2 teaspoons finely chopped walnuts, toasted

Combine first 4 ingredients in a bowl; stir well. Cover and chill.

Cut pears in half lengthwise; core and cut lengthwise into thin slices. Arrange pears on each of 4 radicchio-lined salad plates. Drizzle each with 2 tablespoons yogurt mixture; sprinkle with cheese and walnuts. Yield: 4 servings.

PER SERVING: 145 CALORIES (25% FROM FAT)
FAT 4.0G (SATURATED FAT 1.7G)
PROTEIN 4.3G   CARBOHYDRATE 25.7G
CHOLESTEROL 8MG   SODIUM 156MG

Southwestern Bean and Pasta Salad

To serve this salad cold, chill the pasta mixture and dressing separately. Combine just before serving to keep the pasta from absorbing all the dressing.

8 ounces rotini (corkscrew pasta), uncooked
1 cup frozen whole-kernel corn, thawed
½ cup diced sweet red pepper
½ cup diced purple onion
½ cup minced fresh cilantro
1 (16-ounce) can dark red kidney beans, drained
1 (4½-ounce) can chopped green chiles
¾ cup nonfat mayonnaise
2 tablespoons cider vinegar
2 teaspoons chili powder
1 teaspoon ground cumin
¼ teaspoon salt
¼ teaspoon pepper
1 large clove garlic, minced

Cook pasta according to package directions, omitting salt and fat. Drain; rinse with cold water, and drain again. Place pasta in a large bowl. Add corn and next 5 ingredients; toss well.

Combine mayonnaise and next 6 ingredients, stirring well. Pour mayonnaise mixture over pasta mixture; toss well. Yield: 8 (1-cup) servings.

PER SERVING: 225 CALORIES (4% FROM FAT)
FAT 0.9G (SATURATED FAT 0.1G)
PROTEIN 9.7G   CARBOHYDRATE 45.7G
CHOLESTEROL 0MG   SODIUM 537MG

Mostaccioli Pizza Salad

MOSTACCIOLI PIZZA SALAD

1½ cups mostaccioli (tubular pasta), uncooked
3 tablespoons white vinegar
2 tablespoons water
1 tablespoon olive oil
¾ teaspoon dried Italian seasoning
¼ teaspoon salt
¼ teaspoon pepper
2 cloves garlic, crushed
1 cup sliced fresh mushrooms
¾ cup cherry tomatoes, quartered
½ cup chopped green pepper
½ cup (2 ounces) shredded part-skim
　　mozzarella cheese
Cherry tomatoes (optional)

Cook pasta according to package directions, omitting salt and fat. Drain and set aside.

Combine vinegar and next 6 ingredients in a medium bowl, stirring with a wire whisk until blended. Add pasta, mushrooms, tomatoes, green pepper, and cheese; toss gently to coat. Cover and chill. Garnish with additional cherry tomatoes, if desired. Yield: 5 (1-cup) servings.

PER SERVING: 164 CALORIES (28% FROM FAT)
FAT 5.2G (SATURATED FAT 1.6G)
PROTEIN 6.6G   CARBOHYDRATE 22.3G
CHOLESTEROL 7MG   SODIUM 174MG

Vichyssoise Potato Salad

VICHYSSOISE POTATO SALAD

10 medium-size unpeeled round red potatoes
    (about 3 pounds)
1½ tablespoons olive oil
2 cups coarsely chopped leeks (about 3 medium)
¾ cup sliced green onions
½ cup chopped fresh parsley
¼ cup diced pimiento
½ cup plain low-fat yogurt
3 tablespoons white wine vinegar
1 tablespoon Dijon mustard
½ teaspoon salt
½ teaspoon pepper
¼ teaspoon dried tarragon

Place potatoes in a large Dutch oven. Cover with water; bring to a boil. Partially cover, reduce heat, and simmer 25 minutes or until tender. Drain; let potatoes cool.

Heat oil in a large nonstick skillet over medium heat. Add leeks, and sauté 5 minutes or until lightly browned.

Cut potatoes into ¼-inch slices. Combine potato slices, leeks, green onions, parsley, and pimiento in a large bowl. Combine yogurt and next 5 ingredients in a bowl; stir well. Add to potato mixture, tossing gently to coat. Cover and chill. Yield: 8 (1-cup) servings.

PER SERVING: 198 CALORIES (15% FROM FAT)
FAT 3.3G (SATURATED FAT 0.6G)
PROTEIN 5.5G   CARBOHYDRATE 38.0G
CHOLESTEROL 1MG   SODIUM 235MG

HOT-AND-SOUR SPINACH SALAD

¼ cup fine, dry breadcrumbs
⅛ teaspoon salt
4 ounces reduced-fat Monterey Jack cheese, cubed
1 egg white, lightly beaten
6 cups torn fresh spinach
½ cup sliced green onions
3 tablespoons brown sugar
¼ cup plus 2 tablespoons canned vegetable or chicken broth, undiluted
3 tablespoons balsamic vinegar
½ teaspoon hot sauce
2 large pink grapefruit, peeled and sectioned

Combine breadcrumbs and salt; stir well. Dip cheese in egg white; dredge in breadcrumb mixture. Place cheese on a baking sheet lined with wax paper. Freeze 30 minutes.

Combine spinach and green onions; toss well, and set aside.

Combine brown sugar and next 3 ingredients in a small saucepan; stir well. Bring to a boil; remove from heat, and stir in grapefruit.

Remove prepared cheese from freezer. Remove wax paper, and bake cheese at 400° for 3 to 4 minutes or until cheese begins to soften.

Pour grapefruit mixture over spinach mixture; toss. Top with baked cheese. Yield: 6 servings.

PER SERVING: 133 CALORIES (28% FROM FAT)
FAT 4.1G (SATURATED FAT 2.2G)
PROTEIN 8.4G   CARBOHYDRATE 17.1G
CHOLESTEROL 12MG   SODIUM 317MG

ITALIAN GREEN SALAD

Regular crumbled feta cheese is a tasty substitute for basil-tomato feta cheese.

1 cup frozen artichoke hearts, thawed
¼ cup plus 2 tablespoons commercial oil-free Italian dressing
1 tablespoon red wine vinegar
¼ teaspoon dry mustard
2 cups torn red leaf lettuce
2 cups torn romaine lettuce
1 cup pear-shaped cherry tomatoes, halved
½ small purple onion, sliced and separated into rings
¼ cup crumbled basil- and tomato-flavored feta cheese

Place artichoke hearts in a heavy-duty, zip-top plastic bag. Combine Italian dressing, vinegar, and mustard, stirring well with a wire whisk. Spoon 2 tablespoons dressing mixture over artichokes. Seal bag, and shake until artichokes are well coated. Marinate in refrigerator 1 hour. Remove artichokes from marinade, discarding marinade.

Combine artichokes, lettuces, tomatoes, and onion. Add remaining dressing mixture, and toss well. Place 1¼ cups lettuce mixture on each individual salad plate. Sprinkle with feta cheese. Yield: 4 (1¼-cup) servings.

PER SERVING: 75 CALORIES (29% FROM FAT)
FAT 2.4G (SATURATED FAT 1.4G)
PROTEIN 3.6G   CARBOHYDRATE 11.2G
CHOLESTEROL 8MG   SODIUM 368MG

Food Facts

Feta cheese is produced not only in its native Greece but also in the United States, and it's available in most supermarkets. Domestic brands are packaged in plastic containers without brine and are available in various flavors, such as feta with basil and tomato. Be aware that feta is not known for its meltability—it will retain its crumbly texture even after cooking. American-made feta has approximately 3 grams less fat per ounce than regular Cheddar cheese.

VEGETABLE-BARLEY CASSEROLE

Barley is a good source of fiber. Serve it as a side dish, or stir it into soups, stews, and casseroles.

1 tablespoon reduced-calorie margarine
1½ cups sliced fresh mushrooms
¾ cup pearl barley, uncooked
⅓ cup chopped onion
2 tablespoons chopped fresh parsley
1 cup thinly sliced zucchini, halved
½ cup shredded carrot
1 (14½-ounce) can vegetable broth
½ teaspoon pepper

Melt margarine in a nonstick skillet over medium-high heat. Add mushrooms and next 3 ingredients; sauté 5 minutes or until barley is lightly browned. Place barley mixture, zucchini, and carrot in a 1½-quart baking dish.

Bring broth to a boil in a saucepan; pour hot broth over barley mixture, stirring gently. Stir in pepper. Cover and bake at 350° for 45 minutes or until barley is tender and liquid is absorbed. Yield: 8 servings.

Note: If desired, you may substitute 1 (14½-ounce) can chicken broth for the vegetable broth.

PER SERVING: 99 CALORIES (14% FROM FAT)
FAT 1.5G (SATURATED FAT 0.2G)
PROTEIN 2.8G CARBOHYDRATE 19.8G
CHOLESTEROL 0MG SODIUM 238MG

SEASONED COUSCOUS

Vegetable cooking spray
½ teaspoon peanut oil
¼ cup sliced green onions
½ cup canned vegetable or chicken broth, undiluted
¼ cup water
½ cup couscous, uncooked
2 teaspoons low-sodium soy sauce
⅓ cup peeled, seeded, and chopped tomato
1 tablespoon chopped fresh parsley
¼ to ½ teaspoon freshly ground pepper
1 plum tomato (optional)
½ teaspoon whole peppercorns (optional)

Coat a medium saucepan with cooking spray; add oil. Place over medium-high heat until hot. Add green onions, and sauté until tender.

Add vegetable broth and water; bring to a boil. Remove from heat. Add couscous and soy sauce; cover and let stand 5 minutes. Stir in chopped tomato, parsley, and pepper.

If garnish is desired, cut top third from plum tomato; discard. Use a paring knife to make decorative cuts around edge of tomato; place peppercorns in center. Yield: 4 (½-cup) servings.

PER SERVING: 93 CALORIES (11% FROM FAT)
FAT 1.1G (SATURATED FAT 0.1G)
PROTEIN 3.1G CARBOHYDRATE 18.0G
CHOLESTEROL 0MG SODIUM 300MG

Quick Tip

Need a really quick side dish? Try couscous, a tiny, beadlike pasta that has its origin in the Middle East and North Africa. Just add dry couscous to a pan of boiling water; cover pan, and remove from heat. In only 5 minutes, the couscous is done! Or try cooking it in a broth seasoned with herbs and spices for added flavor as in the Seasoned Couscous above.

Seasoned Couscous

MUSHROOM RISOTTO

1⅔ cups canned vegetable or chicken broth,
       undiluted
1⅔ cups water
Vegetable cooking spray
1 tablespoon margarine
¼ pound sliced fresh mushrooms
2 green onions, sliced
1 cup Arborio rice, uncooked
2 tablespoons freshly grated Parmesan cheese

Combine broth and water in a small saucepan;
cover and bring to a simmer. Keep broth warm over
low heat. (Do not boil.)

Coat a large skillet with cooking spray; add margarine, and place over medium heat until margarine
melts. Add mushrooms and green onions, and sauté
until tender. Add rice; cook over medium heat 2
minutes, stirring constantly.

Add ½ cup of the simmering broth to rice mixture, and cook, stirring constantly, until most of the
liquid is absorbed. Add remaining broth, ½ cup at a
time, cooking and stirring constantly until each ½
cup addition is absorbed. (Rice will be tender and
will have a creamy consistency. The total cooking
time should be about 30 minutes.) To serve, add
Parmesan cheese, and toss. Yield: 6 servings.

PER SERVING: 152 CALORIES (20% FROM FAT)
FAT 3.4G (SATURATED FAT 0.8G)
PROTEIN 3.5G   CARBOHYDRATE 27.4G
CHOLESTEROL 2MG   SODIUM 338MG

WILD RICE WITH PINE NUTS

1 cup canned vegetable or chicken broth,
      undiluted
1 cup water
1 cup chopped onion
½ cup wild rice, uncooked
½ cup brown rice, uncooked
3 tablespoons pine nuts, toasted
1 teaspoon pepper
1 teaspoon dried basil

Combine first 5 ingredients in a medium saucepan; bring to a boil. Cover, reduce heat, and simmer 30 minutes. Stir in toasted pine nuts, pepper,
and basil. Cover and simmer an additional 15 minutes or until rice is tender and liquid is absorbed.
Yield: 6 (½-cup) servings.

PER SERVING: 158 CALORIES (29% FROM FAT)
FAT 5.1G (SATURATED FAT 0.8G)
PROTEIN 4.3G   CARBOHYDRATE 26.0G
CHOLESTEROL 0MG   SODIUM 178MG

PENNE PASTA WITH TOMATOES

5 ripe plum tomatoes, seeded and cut into
      ½-inch pieces
½ cup chopped fresh basil
¼ cup halved ripe olives
1 clove garlic, minced
1½ tablespoons olive oil
1 tablespoon balsamic vinegar
⅛ teaspoon salt
⅛ teaspoon coarsely ground pepper
6 ounces penne (short tubular pasta),
      uncooked
¼ cup crumbled feta cheese

Combine first 8 ingredients in a medium bowl;
toss well. Cover and let stand 15 minutes.

Cook pasta according to package directions, omitting salt and fat; drain well. Add pasta to tomato
mixture; toss gently. Transfer to a serving dish;
sprinkle with feta cheese. Yield: 10 (½-cup)
servings.

PER SERVING: 105 CALORIES (30% FROM FAT)
FAT 3.5G (SATURATED FAT 0.8G)
PROTEIN 3.1G   CARBOHYDRATE 15.4G
CHOLESTEROL 3MG   SODIUM 96MG

Penne Pasta with Tomatoes

ASPARAGUS DIJON

1½ pounds fresh asparagus spears
1 tablespoon cornstarch
1 cup nonfat buttermilk
2 teaspoons Dijon mustard
¾ teaspoon lemon juice
½ teaspoon dried tarragon
¼ teaspoon ground white pepper

Snap off tough ends of asparagus. Remove scales from spears with a knife or vegetable peeler, if desired. Arrange asparagus in a vegetable steamer over boiling water. Cover and steam 7 minutes or until crisp-tender. Set aside, and keep warm.

Combine cornstarch and buttermilk in a small saucepan; stir well. Cook over medium heat until thickened and bubbly, stirring constantly. Remove from heat; stir in mustard, lemon juice, tarragon, and white pepper.

Arrange asparagus on a serving platter. Spoon sauce over asparagus. Serve immediately. Yield: 6 servings.

PER SERVING: 42 CALORIES (11% FROM FAT)
FAT 0.5G (SATURATED FAT 0.1G)
PROTEIN 4.1G   CARBOHYDRATE 6.5G
CHOLESTEROL 0MG   SODIUM 94MG

ROASTED GREEN BEANS AND ONIONS

1 pound fresh green beans
1 small purple onion, sliced and separated into rings
4 large cloves garlic, cut in half lengthwise
Olive-oil flavored cooking spray
½ teaspoon dried thyme
¼ teaspoon salt
¼ teaspoon freshly ground pepper

Wash beans; trim ends, and remove strings. Place beans, onion, and garlic in a 13- x 9- x 2-inch baking pan coated with cooking spray. Coat vegetables with cooking spray. Sprinkle thyme and salt over vegetables; toss well.

Bake at 450° for 15 minutes or until tender, stirring once. Sprinkle with pepper. Yield: 4 (¾-cup) servings.

PER SERVING: 54 CALORIES (8% FROM FAT)
FAT 0.5G (SATURATED FAT 0.0G)
PROTEIN 2.5G   CARBOHYDRATE 11.8G
CHOLESTEROL 0MG   SODIUM 156MG

CURRIED GREEN BEANS AND POTATOES

1 pound unpeeled, small round red potatoes, halved and sliced (about 3 cups)
2½ cups (1-inch) sliced fresh green beans
1½ teaspoons curry powder
½ teaspoon salt
½ teaspoon cumin seeds, crushed
¼ teaspoon ground ginger
⅛ teaspoon pepper
1 cup plain low-fat yogurt
1 clove garlic, minced
1 tablespoon chopped, unsalted dry-roasted peanuts

Place potato slices in a medium saucepan; cover with water, and bring to a boil over medium-high heat. Cover and cook 5 minutes. Add green beans, and cook, uncovered, 8 minutes or until vegetables are tender. Drain and set aside.

Combine curry powder and next 4 ingredients in a large nonstick skillet; cook over low heat 5 minutes. Stir in yogurt and minced garlic; cook just until mixture is warm. (Do not overcook or yogurt will separate.)

Combine potato mixture and yogurt mixture in a large bowl; toss gently. Sprinkle with peanuts. Yield: 6 (1-cup) servings.

PER SERVING: 110 CALORIES (13% FROM FAT)
FAT 1.6G (SATURATED FAT 0.5G)
PROTEIN 4.9G   CARBOHYDRATE 20.4G
CHOLESTEROL 2MG   SODIUM 230MG

Curried Green Beans and Potatoes

Broccoli-Rice Casserole

BROCCOLI-RICE CASSEROLE

3 cups chopped fresh broccoli
1 tablespoon plus 2 teaspoons stick margarine,
    divided
¼ cup chopped onion
3 tablespoons all-purpose flour
½ teaspoon dry mustard
1¼ cups skim milk
⅛ teaspoon pepper
1¾ cups cooked long-grain rice (cooked
    without salt or fat)
1 cup (4 ounces) shredded reduced-fat sharp
    Cheddar cheese
¼ cup nonfat mayonnaise
Vegetable cooking spray
⅓ cup crushed unsalted melba toast (about
    5 slices)

Cook chopped broccoli in boiling water 3 minutes or until crisp-tender. Drain and plunge into cold water; drain again. Set aside.

Melt 1 tablespoon plus 1 teaspoon margarine in a medium saucepan over medium heat; add onion, and sauté 3 minutes or until tender. Add flour and mustard; cook 1 minute, stirring constantly with a wire whisk. Gradually add milk, stirring constantly. Cook an additional 2 minutes or until thickened and bubbly, stirring constantly. Remove from heat; stir in pepper.

Combine broccoli, milk mixture, rice, cheese, and mayonnaise in a bowl; stir well. Spoon into a shallow 2-quart baking dish coated with cooking spray.

Melt remaining 1 teaspoon margarine, and combine with melba toast crumbs; sprinkle over broccoli mixture. Bake at 350° for 25 minutes or until thoroughly heated. Yield: 8 (½-cup) servings.

PER SERVING: 161 CALORIES (31% FROM FAT)
FAT 5.6G (SATURATED FAT 2.1G)
PROTEIN 8.0G   CARBOHYDRATE 20.2G
CHOLESTEROL 10MG   SODIUM 271MG

ITALIAN EGGPLANT AND RICE

If you use regular rice instead of converted long-grain rice in this recipe, the cooking time may vary slightly.

Vegetable cooking spray
1 teaspoon olive oil
3¾ cups cubed eggplant
2 cups chopped green pepper
1 cup diced onion
2 cloves garlic, minced
½ cup converted long-grain rice, uncooked
½ cup minced fresh parsley
1 cup water
1 cup no-salt-added tomato sauce
1 (4½-ounce) can chopped green chiles
1 (4-ounce) jar diced pimiento, drained
2 tablespoons capers
2 tablespoons no-salt-added tomato paste
1 tablespoon balsamic vinegar
1 teaspoon dried Italian seasoning
1 teaspoon sugar
¼ teaspoon dried crushed red pepper
1 tablespoon freshly grated Parmesan cheese

Coat a large Dutch oven with cooking spray; add olive oil. Place over medium-high heat until hot. Add eggplant and next 3 ingredients; sauté 8 to 10 minutes or until vegetables are tender. Reduce heat to low; cook, uncovered, 20 minutes, stirring frequently.

Add rice and next 11 ingredients; bring to a boil over medium-high heat. Cover, reduce heat, and simmer 20 minutes or until rice is tender, stirring occasionally. Sprinkle with Parmesan cheese. Yield: 5 (1-cup) servings.

PER SERVING: 167 CALORIES (10% FROM FAT)
FAT 1.9G (SATURATED FAT 0.4G)
PROTEIN 4.7G   CARBOHYDRATE 34.6G
CHOLESTEROL 0MG   SODIUM 466MG

PEAS AND CAULIFLOWER IN YOGURT-CUMIN SAUCE

¾ pound fresh English peas
2 cups water
4 cups small cauliflower flowerets
¼ teaspoon salt
¾ cup plain low-fat yogurt
3 tablespoons chopped fresh cilantro
1 tablespoon lemon juice
¼ teaspoon ground cumin
Dash of ground white pepper

   Shell and wash peas. Bring 2 cups water to a boil
in a large saucepan; add peas and cauliflower.
Cover and cook 7 minutes or until crisp-tender;
drain well, and place in a bowl. Add salt; toss well.
   Combine yogurt and next 4 ingredients; stir well.

Pour over cauliflower mixture; toss gently. Yield: 4
(1-cup) servings.

PER SERVING: 83 CALORIES (11% FROM FAT)
FAT 1.0G (SATURATED FAT 0.5G)
PROTEIN 6.4G   CARBOHYDRATE 13.9G
CHOLESTEROL 3MG   SODIUM 195MG

SUCCOTASH

2 cups shelled fresh lima beans
2 cups corn cut from cob (about 4 ears)
3 tablespoons reduced-calorie margarine
¼ cup finely chopped onion
2 tablespoons chopped fresh parsley
¼ teaspoon salt
⅛ teaspoon pepper

   Place lima beans in a large saucepan, and add
water to cover; bring to a boil. Cover, reduce heat,

Peas and Cauliflower in Yogurt-Cumin Sauce

and simmer 10 minutes. Add corn; cover and cook 7 minutes or until beans are tender. Drain well.

Melt margarine in saucepan over medium-high heat. Add onion, and sauté 2 minutes. Remove from heat. Stir in lima bean mixture, parsley, salt, and pepper. Yield: 4 (1-cup) servings.

PER SERVING: 197 CALORIES (26% FROM FAT)
FAT 5.8G (SATURATED FAT 1.0G)
PROTEIN 8.1G   CARBOHYDRATE 31.5G
CHOLESTEROL 0MG   SODIUM 270MG

POTATO GNOCCHI

1 pound unpeeled round red potatoes (about
   3 medium)
1 teaspoon olive oil
1 clove garlic, minced
¾ cup all-purpose flour
½ teaspoon salt
Vegetable cooking spray

Place potatoes in a saucepan; add water to cover. Bring to a boil; partially cover. Cook 40 minutes or until tender. Drain and let cool. Peel potatoes, and place in a bowl; mash. Set aside.

Heat oil in a small nonstick skillet over medium-high heat. Add garlic, and sauté 30 seconds. Add to mashed potato; stir well. Add flour and salt, stirring to form a soft dough.

Turn dough out onto a well-floured surface. Divide dough into 4 portions, and shape each portion into a 16-inch-long rope. Cut each rope into 16 (1-inch) pieces; roll each piece into a ball. Drag the tines of a fork through half of each ball, forming a concave shape. Place gnocchi on a baking sheet coated with cooking spray, and set aside.

Bring 14 cups water to a boil in a large Dutch oven. Add half of the gnocchi, and cook 1½ minutes. (Do not overcook or gnocchi will fall apart.) Remove gnocchi with a slotted spoon, and place in a colander to drain; repeat procedure with the remaining gnocchi. Yield: 4 servings.

PER SERVING: 175 CALORIES (8% FROM FAT)
FAT 1.6G (SATURATED FAT 0.2G)
PROTEIN 4.8G   CARBOHYDRATE 35.5G
CHOLESTEROL 0MG   SODIUM 302MG

BASIL VARIATION

Add ⅓ cup finely chopped fresh basil to mashed potato with flour and salt.

SPINACH VARIATION (GNOCCHI VERDE)

Add 1½ cups finely chopped fresh spinach to mashed potato with flour and salt.

SPINACH-RICE TIMBALES

1 (10-ounce) package frozen chopped spinach,
   thawed and drained
⅔ cup 1% low-fat cottage cheese
½ cup plain nonfat yogurt
¼ cup (1 ounce) crumbled feta cheese
¼ teaspoon salt
¼ teaspoon dried basil
¼ teaspoon coarsely ground pepper
2 eggs
2 egg whites
¾ cup cooked long-grain rice (cooked without
   salt or fat)
Vegetable cooking spray

Press spinach between paper towels until barely moist; set aside.

Combine cottage cheese and next 7 ingredients in a bowl; beat at medium speed of an electric mixer until blended. Stir in spinach and rice.

Divide mixture among 6 (6-ounce) custard cups coated with cooking spray. Place cups in a large baking pan; add hot water to pan to a depth of 1 inch. Bake at 350° for 40 minutes or until a knife inserted near center comes out clean. Remove cups from water; loosen edges of timbales with a knife or rubber spatula. Place a serving plate upside down on top of each cup; invert timbale onto plate. Serve warm. Yield: 6 servings.

PER SERVING: 112 CALORIES (26% FROM FAT)
FAT 3.2G (SATURATED FAT 1.4G)
PROTEIN 10.0G   CARBOHYDRATE 10.8G
CHOLESTEROL 76MG   SODIUM 341MG

PROVENÇALE STUFFED TOMATOES

4 medium unpeeled tomatoes (about 1¾ pounds)
1 teaspoon olive oil
Vegetable cooking spray
¾ cup chopped onion
2 large cloves garlic, minced
2 tablespoons chopped fresh parsley
1 teaspoon chopped fresh basil
1 teaspoon chopped fresh thyme
¼ teaspoon salt
⅛ teaspoon pepper
½ cup fine, dry breadcrumbs
2 tablespoons plus 2 teaspoons freshly grated Parmesan cheese

Cut tops off tomatoes; discard. Carefully scoop pulp into a bowl, leaving shells intact. Coarsely chop pulp, and set aside.

Heat oil over medium-high heat in a medium nonstick skillet coated with cooking spray. Add onion and garlic, and sauté 1½ minutes or until tender. Stir in tomato pulp, parsley, and next 4 ingredients; sauté 3 minutes or until moisture evaporates. Remove from heat; stir in breadcrumbs.

Stuff tomato shells with breadcrumb mixture; sprinkle each with 2 teaspoons cheese. Place stuffed tomatoes in a small baking dish. Bake, uncovered, at 375° for 15 minutes or until cheese melts. Yield: 4 servings.

PER SERVING: 126 CALORIES (26% FROM FAT)
FAT 3.7G (SATURATED FAT 1.2G)
PROTEIN 5.1G   CARBOHYDRATE 19.6G
CHOLESTEROL 4MG   SODIUM 333MG

VEGETABLE-STUFFED ZUCCHINI

(pictured on page 118)

4 medium zucchini (about 1½ pounds)
¾ cup finely chopped tomato
⅓ cup chopped green pepper
¼ cup chopped onion
¼ teaspoon salt
¼ teaspoon dried basil
¼ teaspoon dried oregano
⅓ cup (1.3 ounces) shredded reduced-fat Cheddar cheese

Place zucchini in a large saucepan with water to cover. Bring to a boil; cover, reduce heat, and simmer 4 to 6 minutes or until crisp-tender. Drain and let cool.

Cut zucchini in half lengthwise. Scoop out pulp, leaving ¼-inch-thick shells. Chop pulp; reserve shells.

Combine zucchini pulp, tomato, and next 5 ingredients; stir well. Spoon into zucchini shells. Place shells in a 13- x 9- x 2-inch baking dish. Bake, uncovered, at 400° for 15 minutes. Sprinkle with cheese. Bake an additional 5 minutes or until cheese melts. Yield: 8 servings.

PER SERVING: 34 CALORIES (29% FROM FAT)
FAT 1.1G (SATURATED FAT 0.6G)
PROTEIN 2.6G   CARBOHYDRATE 4.3G
CHOLESTEROL 3MG   SODIUM 112MG

FYI

Fresh vegetables reward you with the fullest flavors, the most nutrients, and usually the best prices. Concentrate on buying vegetables that are in season. Not only will they be at their peak of quality and flavor, they will also be available at the most reasonable prices.

When buying fresh vegetables, look for freshness and crispness. Avoid vegetables that have soft or bruised spots. Often a bad spot on just one item will cause spoilage among the rest.

INDEX